Praise for

The Space Between: A Memoir of Mother-Daughter Love at the End of Life

"A stunning, honest book about a mother and daughter at the end of life. Even as a Bereavement Care Specialist, Virginia Simpson was unprepared for the challenges and emotions inherent in caregiving. *The Space Between* offers hope to us all that despite struggles, misunderstandings, and hurt feelings, when two people are honest and never give up, love can heal even the most contentious relationship. This is a must-read: Touching, insightful, painful, and uplifting."
—**Claire Bidwell Smith,** author of *The Rules of Inheritance*

"*The Space Between* is a moving evocation of grief therapist Virginia Simpson's emotional bond with her aging mother, Ruth, and a poignant, clear-eyed account of her journey as Ruth's caregiver during the last years of her life. In warm but unsparingly honest words, Simpson traces the many painful threads of her relationship with her mother--their shared grief over her father's untimely death, their conflicts over the abuse Simpson had suffered at the hands of her brother, and their fear and resentment as the balance of power, tipped by Ruth's failing health, inexorably shifted from mother to daughter. Just as honestly, she captures the deep underlying love, admiration and respect that she and her mother felt for one another--love that they found ways to express even in the midst of their pain. Some scenes in this book will inspire a shudder of recognition in readers who are or have been a parent's caregiver; others recall the sense of mystery that attends

the end of a parent's life, and the grief that follows. Simpson's memoir offers a testament to love's enduring and transformative power throughout our lives and in our closest family ties."
—**Diane Guernsey,** Executive Editor, *Pulse—voices from the heart of medicine* (www.pulsevoices.org)

"A beautiful, searingly honest book about the exhausting, yet rewarding, experience of being an end-of-life caretaker. Virginia Simpson was her mother's primary caretaker for the last six years of her mother's life and, in scenes that will be familiar to daughters and mothers everywhere, the two of them argue, rehash the past, clash and forgive one another and ultimately reach a place of deep love and healing. A must-read for daughters and mothers at all phases of life. Moving, insightful and uplifting."
—**Zoe FitzGerald Carter,** author of *Imperfect Endings: A Daughter's Story of Love, Loss, and Letting Go* (Simon & Schuster)

"*The Space Between* is an unflinching look at end of life, and in particular, the final days of one mother-daughter relationship. The tables turn on Bereavement Specialist Virginia Simpson when she is cast as caregiver for her mother and must reflect on her life's work from a new and highly emotional vantage point. A poignant read."
—**Lynne Griffin,** author of the novels *Girl Sent Away, Sea Escape, Life Without Summer,* and the nonfiction parenting guide, *Negotiation Generation*

"I found so much to connect with in Virginia Simpson's poignant memoir of loving and caring for her mother, Ruth, during her final years. By exploring her own conflicted thoughts and feelings, Simpson gives tacit encouragement for other adult children to do the same. *The Space Between* shows us that growing older requires bravery and determination, as does caregiving. When we're willing to speak honestly about the challenges on both sides, it can put us on the path towards a deeper connection with our parents, and our true selves."

—**Judith Henry,** author of *The Dutiful Daughter's Guide to Caregiving*

"In Virginia Simpson's memoir, *The Space Between*, we're invited into the intimate story of a mother and daughter in the waning years of their relationship, marked by misunderstandings often experienced by adult mothers and daughters. We follow her as she attends her mother's end of life journey. Despite Simpson's career and expertise with death and dying, she finds her mother's decline painful and illuminating in ways she couldn't imagine. As we walk in her shoes, we discover how conscious tending and moment-by-moment compassion create transformation and healing for them both, allowing them to say goodbye with love."

—**Linda Joy Myers,** President of the National Association of Memoir Writers and author of *Don't Call Me Mother*

"*The Space Between* spoke deeply into parts of my soul and psyche: the bereft, sometimes angry, daughter; the grief expert who was struggling with caregiving; the little girl who ached for an emotionally available parent; the adult daughter who learned forgiveness and compassion. Virginia Simpson's vulnerability and transparency will walk you into spaces we often hold private; ones that when spoken aloud, unite and free us."

—**Susan Salluce,** MA, CT, author of *griefINK* & *Out of Breath*

"Finally, a memoir of a mother and daughter's love at end of life. *The Space Between* is a beautiful story that promises to stimulate a

conversation about a daughter's role during an aging mother's end-of-life experience and the significance of compassionate healthcare professionals during that time. The strength of *The Space Between* is that even though mothers and daughters may feel guilt, self-doubt, shame, frayed, worried, scared, frustrated, drained, overwhelmed, or humiliated, at the end of life, all they want to feel is love."
—**Barbara Rubel,** MS, BCETS, author of *But I Didn't Say Goodbye*

"Many of us will face the confusion and heartbreak of helping elderly loved ones through their last days. In *The Space Between*, Dr. Virginia Simpson, an acclaimed bereavement care specialist, not only shares her own journey, but also focuses a lens on her difficult and evolving relationship with her aging mother. An empowering memoir, The Space Between is filled with insights and wisdom about this most human of experiences."
—**Lynne Morgan Spreen,** author of the award winning *Dakota Blue*

"*The Space Between* is a thought-provoking and moving recollection of the final journey a daughter takes with her mother when forced to face the inevitability of mortality. It is about bridging the gap between generations, ones capacity for love and forgiveness, and personal courage that can be summoned when needed. It is a tale of two women who are headstrong, intelligent, prideful, gracious, forgiving, and bonded by typical mother-daughter love: exasperating, exquisite, eternal. It is an intimate journey of shared lives and history. I was touched by their vulnerability that ultimately led to emotional healing."
—**Kathryn Mattingly,** award winning author of literary suspense novels *Benjamin* and *Journey,* and short story collection *Fractured Hearts.*

THE

SPACE
BETWEEN

THE

SPACE

BETWEEN

A Memoir of Mother-Daughter
Love at the End of Life

....

VIRGINIA A. SIMPSON

SHE WRITES PRESS

Published 2016
Printed in the United States of America
ISBN: 978-1-63152-049-5
Library of Congress Control Number: 2015948661

Interior design by Tabitha Lahr

For information, address:
She Writes Press
1563 Solano Ave #546
Berkeley, CA 94707

She Writes Press is a division of SparkPoint Studio, LLC.

The Space Between is a work of nonfiction. These are the true things that happened,
based on my journal entries and memories. There are no composite characters but
I have chosen to change some names and other distinguishing features in order to
protect the identity and the right to privacy of other people. I have done my best to
tell this story as accurately as possible.

*In memory of my mother, Ruth,
with great love and admiration*

Your Mother is always with you.
She's the whisper of the leaves as you walk down the street.
She's the smell of certain foods you remember, flowers you pick and
perfume that she wore.
She's the cool hand on your brow when you're not feeling well.
She's your breath in the air on a cold winter's day.
She is the sound of the rain that lulls you to sleep, the colors of
a rainbow.
She is Christmas morning.
Your Mother lives inside your laughter.
She's crystallized in every teardrop.
A mother shows every emotion . . . happiness,
sadness, fear, jealousy, love, hate, anger, helplessness, excitement, joy,
sorrow . . . and all the while, hoping and praying
you will only know the good feelings in life.
She's the place you came from, your first home,
and she's the map you follow with every step you take.
She's your first love; your first friend, even your first enemy,
But nothing on earth can separate you.
Not time, not space . . . not even death!

—— Author Unknown

CONTENTS

PART 1 — PRACTICE ROUND

Chapter 1: Day One 1
Chapter 2: Day Two 7
Chapter 3: Day Four 13
Chapter 4: Day Five 18
Chapter 5: Day Seven 25

PART 2 — INTERREGNUM

Chapter 6: Preparation 35
Chapter 7: Home Invasion 46
Chapter 8: First Week 53
Chapter 9: Freedom 60
Chapter 10: No Time to Say Good-Bye 63
Chapter 11: Crossing the Abyss 72
Chapter 12: Thanksgiving 79
Chapter 13: One Millennium is as Good
as The Next 91
Chapter 14: A Slice of Life 100

PART 3 — IN DEATH'S WAITING
ROOM

Chapter 15: True Grit 109
Chapter 16: Nowhere and Everywhere 113

Chapter 17: Oxygen Wars 122

Chapter 18: When Yesterday Becomes Today . . 131

Chapter 19: Little Girl Ninety 144

Chapter 20: Conversations 152

Chapter 21: Hospice 163

Chapter 22: Last Thanksgiving 171

Chapter 23: Not So Merry Christmas 179

Chapter 24: Wake Up! 188

Chapter 25: Caregiver Blues 196

Chapter 26: The Search 208

Chapter 27: Changes 215

Chapter 28: The Blue Wapiti 224

Chapter 29: Have You Been Listening? 234

Chapter 30: The Blue Chip 240

Chapter 31: Echoes of Silence 250

Chapter 32: Perhaps Love 254

Epilogue 262

Acknowledgments 268

Appendix 270

PART 1

PRACTICE ROUND

....

A practice round is played to allow a player to become familiar with a particular course, to differentiate it from the real round. But can one ever prepare for what lies ahead?

Chapter 1:

Practice Round — Day One

It seems to me the best way we can manage the complexities about "mother" is not to remain in judgment of our mothers, no matter how hard that is. If we can find a way to stand in her shoes, and to learn who she was before she was a mother, we may find ourselves seeing her as a whole person, someone who had her own life, her own struggles and problems to solve.

—Linda Joy Myers, May 11, 2014

SUNDAY, JULY 4, 1999

My mother drives me crazy. She can send me from love to exasperation faster than my Uncle Henry's Jaguar racecar could go from zero to sixty. I'm almost fifty years old, and you'd think by now she couldn't exert this level of power over me.

"Mom, you can't just think about it. You have to call your doctor. A possible blood clot in your leg is nothing to mess around with."

Silence.

Part of me wants to hang up the phone, pack my little-girl red-and-black-plaid plastic suitcase, and run away to oblivion.

I don't run. I stay because she's my mother and she needs me.

It's late afternoon, and inside, thanks to the air conditioner, my home is a cool, comfortable 68 degrees. Outside it's 110, a typical desert summer day in Indian Wells, California. I'm stretched out on my sage-green chenille couch in the miniscule family room across from the kitchen. The ceiling is high, and light pours in through a rectangular window above French doors that overlook the backyard and kidney-shaped swimming pool. Maggie, my eleven-year-old Golden Retriever, lies on the floor next to me. She rests a lot lately, but I don't take notice because I can't remember a time when she wasn't lethargic.

I don't recognize this woman on the phone.

She wasn't always this way. My pragmatic mother could be counted on to handle anything with steady, focused, calm determination. She used to meet life head-on.

When Mom was only forty-seven years old, Dad's sudden death in 1961 left her widowed for a second time. She planned his funeral and, within two weeks, took over as a partner in his furniture factory. A year and a half later, the factory went into bankruptcy because Dad's partner, Leo, understood nothing about business and Mom knew even less. She didn't miss a beat. She dressed in beautiful knit suits and held her head high each day as she went to bankruptcy court. She never once showed a hint of fear or concern about our future. After the trial was over, Mom enrolled in school and began a whole new career as an insurance underwriter. Her courage and determination allowed us to keep our home.

"Mom, give me the doctor's name and number and I'll call him."

"No."

"What do you mean 'no'?"

"No means no. I'm not going to tell you."

Ugh! If I thought it would help I'd bash my head into a wall to alleviate this frustration and release the intense emotions that blow hard inside me as if carried by an impatient windstorm.

Dammit. She's shut the door, sealed the vault, and negotiations are over. Under normal circumstances my mother can out-stubborn me any day of the week, but I'm certain her current situation is unlike anything we've dealt with before. If she thinks she's won this round she is seriously mistaken.

"All right, Mom. Got to go. Call you later."

"Okay, Ginni," she says, her voice relaxed.

"I love you, Mom."

"I love you, too."

I hang up the phone and take a full tour of my home as though examining the furniture and artwork will yield the doctor's name and number. Somehow it works and his last name pops into my head, which is a miracle because I never met the man, and Mom seldom speaks of him. They are in Los Angeles, and I live more than one hundred miles away.

I dash into the bedroom I use as a home office. The simple rectangle of a room contains a narrow three-shelf bookcase, secretarial chair, and long, blond desk that straddles two connecting walls. I slide into the chair, start my Mac, and commence an Internet search for every doctor in Los Angeles with the last name "Green." An unseen something must be with me because I recognize the first name, Marvin, and immediately call him.

"Dr. Green's answering exchange," a smoky professional female voice with a tinge of the South answers after the third ring.

"Please, I need to speak to the doctor. My mother is his patient and I think she has a blood clot in her leg."

"That doesn't sound good. Dr. Harwitt, who works with Dr. Green, is taking his calls tonight. I'll get hold of him right away."

"I appreciate your help." I give her my mother's name and phone number.

"You just relax, honey. I'll take care of everything," the lady's voice, sweet as velvet cake, reassures me. "I'll call him right now."

"Thank you."

I press and release the button on the phone, tap in my mother's number, and stand up. Maggie observes with disinterest as I circle the room while I wait for Mom to answer. As soon as she does, I tell her to expect a call from Dr. Harwitt.

"Oh." She sounds like she just sucked on a lemon.

"Mom, I'm going to get off the phone now so your line won't be busy when he calls. Call me after you talk to him."

As soon as I hang up, I slump down in the chair and lift my hair off my neck to cool down. My shoulders are tense; the tightness stretches up my neck to the bottom of my ear lobes. I press the palms of my hand into my forehead and shake my head to try to get the tension out.

I've done what I can and have to wait. *What if this is it? What if the clot moves and Mom dies?* I've been afraid of this day since Dad died, and now it's here, an unwelcome load of garbage dumped in the middle of my house. *Much as you irritate me, Mom, I'm not ready for you to die!* My eyes fill with hot tears that don't spill but hang like an acrobat balancing on a tightrope. I uncurl my body and sit tall in the chair. I'm my mother's daughter, and we do not fall apart in a crisis.

A sudden loud *boom, bang, crackle* rattles the window above the desk and I leap out of the chair. The rapid beat of my heart thuds hard against my ribs. I forgot it's the 4th of July, and now the firework celebrations have started. When did night fall? I'm alert and jumpy, like I've had too many cups of coffee. I go back into the family room and turn on the TV to distract myself, but the strategy doesn't work. I check the clock every few minutes. An hour seems to crawl by slower than the past decade of my life. I can't stand to wait any longer; I call Mom. Maggie sits by my side and I pet her head while I wait for Mom to answer. One, I'm composed; two, my breath speeds up; three, *Now where the hell is she?;* four, finally, she answers.

"Did you talk to the doctor?"

"Yes, he called." She sounds bored and distracted. I imagine her lips taut and her aquamarine eyes focused and hard with an all-too-familiar look of exasperation.

"What did he say when you told him your symptoms?"

"He said it was nothing to worry about, and I should call Dr. Green's office tomorrow morning and make an appointment."

"Did you tell him about the pain in your groin?"

Silence.

"Ma-om," I whine, like my old teenaged self.

"Virginia, let it go." Her voice is hard as steel, a tone I recognize. She's reestablished herself as the parent and the conversation is closed.

"Okay, Mom, but promise me you'll call Dr. Green's office first thing in the morning."

"I promise."

I don't believe her but don't push the point, and we say good-bye.

I call the doctor's office as soon as we hang up and ask the kind lady with the southern drawl to tell Dr. Harwitt to call me A-S-A-P. Ten minutes later, the phone rings. I grab it on the first ring.

"This is Dr. Harwitt," a pretentious, fustian voice says, and continues before I can respond, "Listen, there's nothing to worry about. Your mother is fine."

Is this guy an idiot? I would like to wring his arrogant neck, but I need him, so I won't let him hear my frustration.

"She's not fine. She has all the symptoms of a blood clot."

"When I spoke to her, she described her symptoms and they did not sound critical to me. She can call Dr. Green tomorrow." He talks the way adults spoke at me when I was a child and they didn't want me around. How often did my parents say, *Children should be seen but not heard?*

I realize I'm not getting through to him, so I end the call with a simple thank-you-and-good-bye. The line goes dead, and for a moment I stand there. The sound of the fireworks has disappeared, and I am surrounded by silence. I scan the room but see nothing. I let Maggie outside to pee, then we pad across the house and into my bedroom, where I change into my sleeveless nightgown, climb into bed, and switch on the TV. Maggie jumps on the bed and cuddles next to me. It's been just Maggie and me alone in this bed for a long time, and I no longer fool myself that having a man in my life would make this evening or what's ahead any easier. I roll over and rest my head on Maggie's body, hoping the drone from the TV will block out my worries and lull me to sleep.

Chapter 2:

Practice Round — Day Two

What you say and do in a crisis matters.

—Ami Bera

MONDAY

I'm awake although my eyes are closed. I dread the thought I'll be in the dark when I open them, so I keep them sealed and hope I can fall back to sleep. Despite the air conditioning, the room is warm due to its thin walls and inefficient vents. I throw the sheets off. The only sound is Maggie's soft, rhythmic breath. I toss and turn, like the princess and the pea, unable to find a comfortable spot. I curl up and stay still as I wait for sweet unconscious sleep to embrace me, but sleep remains distant.

I wonder if my mother is okay. Perhaps this is part of the reason I can't sleep—but the truth is, I can't remember the last time I slept through the night. Probably sometime in the 1980s. I've read that insomnia is common in women once they reach their mid-to-late thirties. I squint over at the clock but the numbers are a blur. I search for my glasses. When I feel the temple, I grab them and slip them on. "Temple" is a funny name for the side-piece that extends from the front of the glasses to the back and around the ears. I always thought of a temple as a place of worship. In a way I do worship my glasses, because they give the gift of sight to my very nearsighted eyes. If only I could see my future.

The clock glares 2:00 a.m. I should have known. It's always 2:00 a.m. when I wake up like this.

I turn on the TV, set the sleep timer to turn off in ninety minutes, and watch a rerun of *The Fresh Prince of Bel-Air*, a sitcom starring Will Smith. The show is not funny, but the sound keeps my mind quiet—finally.

———

Ribbons of sunlight stream into the room through the vertical blinds. I'm groggy, and it's like my head is wrapped in cheesecloth. I'm always in a fog after a broken night's sleep. I check the clock and it's 6:00 a.m., so I get up, pad across the house, scoop coffee into the coffee maker, turn it on, and pad back to the bathroom to start the shower. I try not to look at myself in the mirror while I dry off. Those extra ten pounds are still there, and cellulite is spreading like a virus throughout my chubby thighs. Mom's legs are long and lean with no cellulite, and although she's only five foot three and I'm five foot seven, her legs are longer than mine. Her blue eyes change colors depending on what she wears, sometimes cerulean and other times emerald green. My dark brown eyes remain brown no matter what.

I wait until 8:30 to phone Mom. I pour the last bit of coffee into the sink and put my favorite mug into the dishwasher while I wait for her to answer.

"Did you call the doctor?"

"Yes," she says, her voice robotic, devoid of all emotion.

"And?"

"They say he can get me in late this afternoon."

Dammit! She needs help before then.

"Did you tell him everything?"

"Yes, Virginia, I told him everything." I imagine she purses her perfect lips into a frown.

"Good." I don't trust that she did but decide I won't push the point further, and we say good-bye. Without a second's hesitation, I dash into my office, retrieve the scrap of paper with the doctor's phone number on it, and punch in the numbers. I pace back and forth across the room.

"Dr. Green's office," a girlish voice answers.

I introduce myself and ask to speak to Dr. Green. The girl tells me he's with a patient.

"This is urgent. I must speak to him right away about my mother. Please, get him!" Maybe I bark at her but I don't care. My one last nerve is about to shred, and I am already stripped of all patience.

"One moment, please."

Two minutes go by and a brusque man's voice starts the conversation midsentence— "There is no rush. We've made an appointment for your mother this afternoon at three."

Don't these doctors ever say "hello?"

"Excuse me, Dr. Green. There is a rush." I am determined to jolt him out of his complacency and get my mother into his office. "My mother's leg is swollen and she is experiencing pain in her groin. If my mother says something hurts, then something is *very* wrong. She's been your patient for a long time, so you must be aware my mother *never* complains. You need to see her right away."

Dr. Green's voice lightens and he says, "You're right. Your mother never does complain. I'll tell my nurse to call her as soon as we get off the phone, and we'll fit your mom in the minute she arrives."

"Thank you so much," I say, my voice soft and sweet.

After we hang up, I sit down at my desk and take a few minutes to select an activity for tonight's group for children between the ages of six and twelve who've lost their parents. Four years ago I founded The Mourning Star Center, a nonprofit that provides free support for grieving children and their families, and I lead all the children's groups.

When I've decided on what I believe to be the perfect activity, I call Mom to check on whether the doctor has done as he said he would.

"I'm leaving for the doctor's," she says after I say hello. "I was at the door, on my way out, when the phone rang."

"Okay, Mom. I won't keep you. Call me as soon as you're done. I want to hear what he has to say. Okay?"

She agrees, and after the "I love yous," we hang up.

Two hours later, I stand at the kitchen sink and sip a glass of water as I stare out the window at the brown Santa Rosa Mountains and Ike's Peak (named for President Eisenhower) in the near distance. The heat outside is so intense the air has a density that casts a translucent shroud over the mountains and sky. 108 degrees is unbearable in most places, but in Indian Wells—a small enclave seventeen miles southeast of Palm Springs, California— today is just another summer day. The real heat is still a month off, when temperatures will soar past 115 and never cool down lower than 100, day or night.

My shoulders are hunched high and tight. I have no idea what I think or feel. I'm not in denial. It's just that my mother has always been healthy, and since I've never been in this situation before, I am left with only an ominous sense of what the next few hours are going to bring.

The shrill sound of the phone jolts me out of my reverie. "Hi, Ginni," Mom says when I answer. "I'm in Dr. Green's office, and he's putting me in the hospital immediately." I hold my breath and lean against the counter for support. "He won't even let me go home. He thinks I've got a blood clot in my leg." She sounds like a serious little child—not afraid, just tentative and young. My mom would never tell me she's afraid. She's stoic, which means she never shows sadness or fear. Subdued anger, disdain, and sarcasm are okay for her particular brand of stoicism, but never the softer emotions. Even so, I understand my mother, and I sense the concern below her calm.

"That's what I thought, Mom." My voice is level so she won't hear how tense and scared I am. It was one thing to think she might have a blood clot; knowing her doctor agrees is a whole new level of dreadful reality. "I'm glad he's taking care of you. Which hospital?"

"UCLA."

"Perfect. Call me as soon as you're in a room so you can give me the phone number where I can reach you. I love you."

"Okay. I love you too, honey."

I freeze for a moment, shake my head to clear my thoughts and toss off the inertia. I create a plan of action. For the next few hours, I call everyone I can think of in my search for someone who will watch Maggie and a volunteer to answer the phones and take charge of the children's groups. A girlfriend agrees to take Maggie, but only one volunteer can help, and she's not available until Wednesday.

When Mom calls to gives me the direct phone number to her

hospital room, I tell her I've made arrangements so that I can be there on Wednesday.

"I'm so relieved."

"Why, Mom?"

"I called Peter, and when I told him I expected to be released by Friday and asked if he'd drive me home, he said that he and Ellyn would be away on vacation."

I'm glad Mom can't see my face, as I wouldn't be able to hide the level of disdain I feel towards her firstborn, my older half-brother, Peter.

"I'll be there as long as you need me, Mom."

After we hang up, I feed Maggie and drive the five minutes to the Center in time to meet with my volunteers before the children and their parents come for this evening's group.

⌒

Four hours later, I slide into my white 1994 Lexus. When I turn the ignition key, the radio comes on to the sounds of Ricky Martin's "Livin' La Vida Loca," which is ironic since my world is about to turn into living the crazy life—but without the upbeat, get-off-the-couch-and-dance fun music sung by a cute young Latin male.

I'm beyond exhausted and look forward to being home in my bed with Maggie at my side. I hope I get a good night's sleep.

Chapter 3:

Practice Round — Day Four

A lot of people don't want to make their own decisions.
They're too scared. It's much easier to be told what to do.

—Marilyn Manson

WEDNESDAY

I pause at the doorway. My mother is sitting up in a white hospital bed next to the window at the far side of the room. The typical Los Angeles haze mutes the light of the sun but enough daylight seeps in to make the dull beige room feel less drab. A heavyset lady with curly gray hair snores in the bed closest to the door. Behind me a silver food cart pushed by a woman in green scrubs squeaks through the dreary hallway.

The head and foot of Mom's bed are elevated, and her attention is on the TV set attached to the wall across the room. A silver pole with a hook holds a bag with clear liquid connected by a tube to her left arm. Her arm is dappled with deep purple bruises that make her look as though she has been punched in several places.

Mom doesn't turn as I enter the room, and I wait until I am close before I speak so I won't wake her sleeping roommate.

"Hi, Mom."

She looks weary, and her silver hair is flat and matted in the back. Her blue eyes are glossy and paler than normal, like a washed out sky.

"Hi, honey. I'm glad you're here," she says with a weak smile. The smile reminds me of the smiles I see on the grieving children I work with, smiles that never reach their sad eyes. Despite the tube attached to her arm, she reaches out to me, and I bend over the metal rail on her bed and kiss her cheek, careful not to jostle anything. The white hospital gown with faded blue flowers drowns her tiny frame, and she reminds me of a small, fragile waif.

I walk around to the other side of her bed, pick up the metal chair near the window, and scrape it closer to her.

"How are you feeling?" I ask as I drop into the stiff chair.

"Call the doctor."

"Call the doctor?" My head tilts to the right and my brow furrows. "Why?"

"Just call the doctor." She gestures towards the phone with her eyes, and hands me a scrap of paper with Dr. Green's name and number on it.

"Mom, just tell me what's going on."

She shakes her head, an almost imperceptible motion, and in a soft yet dramatic whisper says, "I can't." She turns her face away from me.

I sigh. "Okay, Mom, I'll call him."

Mom turns back towards me, and I pick up the phone that sits on the nightstand and tap in the numbers. She never takes her eyes off me, but her expression remains inscrutable. If she is scared, and I'm sure she must be, she doesn't let on.

I'm surprised when the doctor, and not his receptionist, answers on the second ring.

I introduce myself and explain that Mom told me to call but wouldn't tell me why.

"I've been waiting for your call."

"What's going on?"

"Your mother has an enormous blood clot, what we call a deep vein thrombosis. The clot starts in the back of her leg and goes up to her inferior vena cava. There are also a few clots in her lungs, but we aren't worried about those. We've put her on a massive infusion of Coumadin, which is a blood thinner."

I can feel my mother watch me. I've got a good poker face, so with no effort on my part, I maintain a neutral expression as I listen to the doctor's words. My mother is also a good poker player, and her thoughts and feelings hide behind a mask of benign patience.

"Clots in her lungs are irrelevant?" I say with all the emotion of one commenting on the weather. Mom's watchful eyes are like a weight and a responsibility. My mind is focused, my face a blank canvas, and my body still. My left palm rests on my chest.

"They are small. The real danger is from the huge clot. No one here has ever seen a blood clot this massive." He pauses.

"Okay, Dr. Green. Go on."

"There's a procedure the hospital didn't want to do because of your mother's advanced age. They figured eighty-four is so old it wouldn't matter if the blood clots kill her, but I pushed hard and was able to convince them to do it. Without the procedure, worst-case scenario, she'll die. Best case, she will never walk again."

The gentle firmness of his voice combined with the honest, forthright manner in which he gives me this ominous informa-

16

tion makes me feel respected as a colleague in my mother's care. I trust him and know we can work together.

"I can't thank you enough, Dr. Green, for going to bat for my mother."

"Thanks are unnecessary. Your mother is still a vibrant woman. The hospital staff doesn't know her so they only looked at her age. I wasn't willing to let them give up on her because of a number."

"Well, I am grateful. Now tell me, what does the procedure entail?" I ask with as much aplomb as I can muster.

"They will go in through the back of her leg and insert a Greenfield stent, which will act as a filter and prevent the clot from moving to her heart, lungs, or brain. You need to understand this procedure is not without serious risk. Although this is her only chance, the procedure could kill her. But I want to be very clear with you. Even if she has the procedure, she can never live alone again." He pauses for a moment and then says, "Your mother told me she wants you to make the decision for her. So, shall we do it?"

What a time for her to hand control over to me! My insides are now in a free fall, my stomach twisting and turning as though my intestines are being squeezed through my grandfather's old-fashioned washing machine wringer, yet my face remains placid and my voice masks my alarm. I'm on autopilot crisis mode, determined to gather all necessary information so I can make a quick decision.

"Dr. Green, did you tell my mother everything you just told me?"

"Yes, of course I did."

"Okay. Let me talk to my mom and get right back to you."

"I'll wait for your call, but don't take long. We need to get her on the schedule as soon as possible." His words are rapid and his voice has gone up half an octave.

After we hang up, I turn my attention to Mom and take her right hand in mine. "What do you want to do?"

She stares at me with the trust a child shows when she knows the parent can and will handle everything and make the world safe.

"You must decide."

I know most people would take their time to think about all this, but I'm an action-oriented person who makes quick decisions once I have all the necessary information. I trust Dr. Green has told me everything I need to know. We are in a battle, and a slow decision could be fatal.

"Well, Mom, I don't see there's a choice. We've got to do what gives you the best chance of life and walking; so I vote for the procedure." I nod my head in assent as I speak these final words.

"Okay," she says without a moment's hesitation.

I suspect she'd already made this decision but wanted to know I agreed.

Our whole discussion about the fate of her life has taken less than a minute. She turns her attention back to the TV and *The Young and the Restless*, her favorite soap opera. I don't know what she feels. Perhaps I'm the carrier of all the worries for both of us, and once she passed the responsibility to me, she let go. My mother is not easy to read, even for me, and I'm the person closest to her in the world.

I wish my suspicions had been wrong, but Mom's symptoms sounded like President Nixon's back in the 1970s when the news announced he had a blood clot in his leg. I paid attention because I had a swollen leg, and when my doctor suspected a blood clot I researched the condition.

I call Dr. Green back and let him know we've decided to go ahead with the stent.

Chapter 4:

Practice Round — Day Five

All women become like their mothers. That is their tragedy.
No man does. That's his.

—Oscar Wilde

THURSDAY

Inside the hospital, it's cool, the air laced with acrid smells of medical chemicals and cleaning fluids. Someone always seems to be mopping a floor. Food carts squeak as they are pushed down the halls, and people on their way to rooms make noise, but I focus all my attention on the soft sound of my mother's breath as she sleeps. The change in Mom's arms since yesterday is a shock. The mottled bruises have spread and congealed into the appearance of midnight-blue or eggplant-purple opera gloves that span the length of her arms.

Outside it's a warm July afternoon and life goes on. People stroll the blocks of Westwood Village, innocent of the dramas and traumas that go on inside this hospital. Those lucky people walk the streets of my youth and happy memories. I've loved Westwood Village my whole life. When we were young, Mom and I would wander these same streets, look into windows, sometimes go inside and buy something, and always stop for lunch. In my twenties and early thirties, I'd come to Westwood to attend classes at UCLA, visit my therapist, go to The Bruin or Village to catch a movie, shop at Bullocks, or meet friends at Café Moustache, where I'd always eat a spinach crepe and chocolate soufflé.

But today there are no strolls, shopping, lunches, movies, classes, or therapy. Today I'm inside this hospital, a place where nothing seems to happen while the most profound aspects of life occur at every moment.

I've been at Mom's side since 10:00 this morning, both of us in loud silence not talking about the procedure scheduled for 4:00 p.m.

When it's time, two young men—one with curly, dark brown hair and a beard, the other a clean-shaven, shaggy-haired blond—wrap a white sheet around Mom and lift her out of the bed with as little effort as it would take to elevate a feather. Their movements are slow and meticulous. With gentle care they place Mom on the slender, stiff gurney. I study their every move from my vantage point on the opposite side of the bed as though my attention will assure they won't drop her. Mom seems teeny, small as a child.

This is a seismic shift in our relationship. Me, the adult; her, the child.

When I was a child and sick with bronchitis, the flu, or any of my other numerous childhood illnesses, Mom was my fantasy mother. I'd lie in my twin bed, huddled under the covers, about to call out for juice or something to eat, and before I could speak, she'd appear as if by magic, with my unspoken wish on the metal tray she held in her manicured hands. My favorite was fresh-cooked chocolate pudding, still warm, with a dark membrane of chocolate on top. I would tunnel under the layer of skin and save that part as a special treat for last.

Mom also brought me gifts. One was a paint-by-numbers set that let me pretend I was the new Rembrandt. Without the set, it was clear I had not inherited Mom's artistic talent. And oh how I loved the books with bright cartoon characters. I read them while a record played the words. *The Tortoise and the Hare* was one of my favorites, with Bugs Bunny starring as the hare and Elmer Fudd as the narrator. A foghorn would tell me when to turn the page. Being sick meant I was safe: Dad didn't yell at me and my older brother didn't hit me. But better than that, it meant I was the focus of Mom's love and attention.

Today it's my turn, and I will not let her down.

I am ragged edges as she is taken away. I hold my body stiff, as though staying rigid will keep everyone safe. I walk in silence next to Mom as they wheel the gurney out of the room. I fight back the urge to jabber as we head down the empty hallway towards the elevator.

The silver doors whine apart as we approach, and I squeeze into a small space at the front of the elevator near the foot of the gurney. One of the men leans down and asks Mom if she's okay. Other than his words and her shallow "yes," we ride the cramped, gray box down in silence. The elevator seems to move at a sloth-like pace while we all focus on the doors in front of us.

Finally, it lurches to a stop and the doors whoosh open to reveal a new bleakness. The underbelly hallways and procedure rooms are stark and austere. The only sounds are the clang of steel instruments, the click of machinery, and the clack of feet in the hallway. Once we're in a small, curtained room on the left at the end of the hall, the young men are replaced by two middle-aged men in white coats—one chubby with black hair specked with white, and the other almost bald with only a few brown sprigs. The bald man stands across from me while the other one sits next to my mother, puts on tortoiseshell half-glasses, and turns his attention to some papers on a clipboard.

"Mrs. Simpson, you're here so we can insert a stent in your leg. There are certain risks in connection with this procedure that I need to go over with you," he reads in a voice devoid of all emotion. He pauses and peers over his glasses at my mother. She watches him, studies him like one would look at something under a microscope. "The doctor is going to implant a Greenfield filter in the back of your leg. In order to do that, we will administer . . ."

I focus on my mother's face and the words fade and trail off like an apparition. My reverie ends when he says—with all the inflection and nuance of someone reading a laundry list—"You could die and . . ."

Die? My mom might die today? I'm not ready. I've always loved my mother even when I didn't like her, but now my love has an urgent intensity. Being this close to her potential death has transformed my feelings for her from a concept into a strong emotional reality. My heart and my life are attached to her at a depth I hadn't realized. I don't want to lose my mom. I can't bear the thought. Why does the fear of loss increase our love?

"What if I don't want to listen to this?" Mom asks.

"Mrs. Simpson," the raven-haired man says with kindness,

"we are legally obligated to advise you about all the risks involved in this procedure."

"Oh," Mom says, then turns her head to the right and promptly falls asleep. Not fake sleep. She is out cold.

I envy this gift. When I'm upset I obsess, overthink, and can't sleep. Insomnia is my middle name. My mother, on the other hand, is a champion sleeper, but I never realized she is able to fall asleep at will when life is unpleasant.

The man doesn't appear to notice that Mom has slipped into sleep. In a soft voice, he continues to read all the horrible things that can go wrong. The words "instant death" linger like a bright neon sign in my head. My breath is shallow and quick.

"Mrs. Simpson, we need you to sign that you were given this information," the tortoiseshell man says.

Mom doesn't stir.

"Can I sign for her?" I ask.

"Not unless she gave you her Power of Attorney."

"No, she didn't." I make a mental note to have her do this if we make it out of here alive.

I lean into Mom and give her arm a gentle shake. "Mom, wake up. We need you to sign something."

A *why'd-you-wake-me* shadow spreads across her face. She gazes up at the man with the innocence of a child, takes the pen he holds out for her, and signs her name in the precise, beautiful penmanship I admire. Even in a crisis, she doesn't allow one letter to drop or be less than perfect.

Tortoiseshell turns to me. "You need to leave now."

"Can I wait down here outside the curtain?"

"No. There are no chairs," he says. "We find it best for family members to wait in the patient's room, where we can reach you should we need to."

I kiss Mom's cheek, and with an upbeat smile on my face and in my voice whisper, "I love you, Mom. See ya soon."

She kisses me and says, "I love you too, honey."

As I turn to go, the tears I've held back fill my eyes. By the time I reach Mom's room, I'm in full control again and my emotions are prisoners locked behind solid steel bars.

The room is empty, and I am alone with only a dull ache for company. I don't know when Mom's roommate checked out, but the bed is empty and stripped of sheets, naked except for the cold indigo pad left behind.

The room seems larger in its emptiness, louder in its silence.

I walk over to the chair next to Mom's bed where I've sat for the past two days. I pick up her paperback copy of *Angela's Ashes* and open to the last page she marked to discover where she is in the book. I never find out. I jump at the sudden, loud, shrill ring of the black phone.

"Hello?"

"How's Mom doing?" Peter asks.

"She's having the procedure now. They say it might kill her." I don't want to listen to my words and acknowledge I said my mother might die.

"Well," he drawls out the word, "I've gotten used to the idea my mother will die. What bothers me is the aftermath." His voice drones, as flat and lifeless as a bad imitation of Boris Karloff. He speaks about the end of our mother's life with the passion one might use to speak about a mere acquaintance.

The emotional ground under me starts to shake. I grasp the bed's rail for stability. An exasperated sigh escapes, but I manage to stifle the urge to tell him off. I turn into The Ice Queen.

"I gotta go. Good-bye," I say and slam the phone down.

Any pretense at stoicism is gone. Peter's indifference to my mother's, to *his* mother's, precarious situation, and my renewed antipathy and disdain towards him explode. I erupt into tears.

I move in frantic strides around the room, each step accentuating the painful edges inside my body. *Asshole. You fucking asshole!* The tears are fierce flames against my cheeks. *She doesn't deserve this!* The room is too small to hold my energy, so I step out into the hall, where I pace some more, all the while mumbling to myself. I'm furious with Peter and terrified Mom will die. The anger and fear have further intensified my love for my mother. It's like a lifetime of love has congealed into something much deeper, or maybe part of me believes I must love her more because Peter appears to care so little. I don't want her to die, and I sob like a baby. *Please, Mom, don't leave me!*

I wish I were anywhere but here in this cold, sterile hospital where death stalks the hallways. I want to be home in the too-hot desert, safe in my warm bedroom, curled up in bed, alone except for Maggie at my side. Even another sleepless night spent thrashing from side to side in the bed would be better than this nightmare day.

As I trounce down the hallway, my heart breaks on my mother's behalf because her son repays her lifetime of loyal, unwavering love for him with a shallow, cavalier attitude towards her survival.

Through my tears, I notice Mom's favorite nurse approach from the other side of the hallway.

"What's wrong?" she asks, her face a reflection of alarm.

I sob out what happened with Peter. I may be screaming, I don't know. I feel like I'm an observer when I say, "She doesn't deserve this! She doesn't deserve this!" As my body crumbles with heavy sobs into the nurse's soft body, her arms wrap around me like a cozy comforter.

Chapter 5:

Practice Round — Day Seven

We are constantly being put to the test by trying circumstances and difficult people and problems not necessarily of our own making.

—Terry Brooks

SATURDAY

Two days later I'm almost at the doorway to Mom's room when the sound of Peter and his wife Ellyn's voices pierce the bubble of my thoughts. All forward movement comes to a halt. I don't want to see them, but when Mom and I spoke this morning I told her I'd be there by 11:00, and I know she'd worry if I didn't show up. I wish I were outside to enjoy the perfect beach weather. I wish it were 1976 and instead of being in this place I was in my bright orange Fiat 124 Sport Spyder with the top down, headed west on Sunset Boulevard past the beautiful mansions lining the tree-filled, curvy street that ends at the Pacific Ocean. I can see myself back then, long brown hair blown by the wind, headed towards Point Dume Beach, a beautiful alcove in Malibu. Few people knew about this secluded spot back then. The radio would be on, and in my memory I hear The Moody Blues "Tuesday Afternoon."

There is no leaving myself behind today, and it's not 1976. Twenty-three years have blazed by, and now it's 1999.

No wishing can change where I am, and as much as I wish I could turn around and walk away, I take the next step into Mom's hospital room.

Mom sits up in her bed, tubes still attached to her arms. She faces Peter and Ellyn, who lean against the wall close to her bed.

Ellyn is in her mid-forties, pretty, with straight black hair and large brown eyes. She's short and chubby, with an ample chest. My mother would use the word *zaftig* to describe her.

Peter is slender and tall at six foot six inches. His blue eyes are veiled in a squint, and his head juts forward from hunched shoulders as though he's not comfortable in his own body. He's bald on top, with a few tenacious brown hairs left on the sides. It's hard to believe the once beautiful boy who wore preppy 1950s V-neck cashmere sweaters and pressed button-down shirts is now this fifty-six-year-old car wreck of a man. His beige clothes are rumpled like he slept in them, rolled out of bed, and came straight to the hospital.

"Hello, Mom," I say with as much cheer as I can muster while I fight the urge to throw up. I stride right over to her, and as I bend to kiss her, she lifts her left cheek towards me, then reaches up and caresses the side of my head above my ear while she kisses me back.

"Hi, honey." She smiles, the first real smile I've seen since she's been in the hospital.

"Hi, Ellyn, Peter," I nod as I squeeze past them.

Peter is so near as I pass, I feel the heat from his body attach to me like a leech. I shudder. I thought I'd forgiven him years ago for abusing me during my childhood. But maybe forgiveness worked only when I didn't have to be in the physical presence of this person who sexually molested me and my best friend when we were seven, beat me on a regular basis throughout my childhood, and made my life hell when I was a teenager. Maybe if he'd ever said he was sorry, maybe if I hadn't heard his cavalier words on Thursday about Mom's life, it might be easier to be in the same room with him. Maybe.

On the outside, I appear as cool as a Mai Tai and focus on my mother. Her arms are still purple with the bruises from the Coumadin and needles. I take a seat next to her bed in what I've come to think of as my chair. Mom continues to watch Peter and Ellyn.

This is the first time I've seen Peter since I told him about Mom's procedure. I've pulled my emotions together and tucked them away in the pocket inside my body where I store unpleasant experiences. I don't know where they go, but I know from my education and years of therapy that when we shove down unpleasantness, it waits to be dealt with at another time, usually in a new relationship with unsuspecting people.

A thick gold chain around Peter's neck holds a free-form pendant made from a web of gold that ensnares a large, blue-gray star sapphire and two diamonds. The gemstones once lived in a platinum ring my father wore on his right pinky finger. When Dad married Mom he legally adopted Peter as his own son. I was born three years later, when Peter was almost seven years old.

The thing around his neck is a bastardization of my father's ring and a sparkling reminder of how my mother chose Peter over me after Dad died. So many years have gone by, and yet the blue of the sapphire reminds me of the years I felt unloved, rejected, betrayed, unimportant, and impotent. Mom spent my Social Security money—death benefits that came from my father—on Peter's Art Center education, and on his twenty-first birthday, she gave him my father's ring without asking me if it was okay.

I know it may sound petty and I shouldn't feel so much outrage, but I do. The ring should have been mine. I loved my father; Peter hated him.

Ellyn talks to Mom as if I'm not there. Mom faces Ellyn and listens. I shift in my seat. Peter fiddles with the necklace.

"Ruth," Ellyn says, "I've told you we've found a place for seniors just a few blocks away from our home." Her voice is stern, like a third grade teacher talking to a child. "We'll be able to visit, bring you groceries, and check on you at least twice a week."

Mom sits very still and says nothing.

My teeth are clenched tight.

In a firm voice, Mom says, "I want to go back to my own apartment."

Ellyn's mouth twists, and she and Peter shuffle in place. Ellyn looks up at him as if to ask his opinion. He frowns but says nothing. I don't understand why Ellyn's still with him or what she sees in him. I wonder if she's forgotten that he hit her the first year they were married.

Ellyn turns to my mother and points at her. "Ruth, you can't. Peter and I've talked, and we think this is the best solution."

I remain silent. I don't want to engage with them and risk an argument. Even though it's been thirty years since Peter last hit me, he has hurt others since then, including both his wives and a girlfriend, and I don't trust him. I can't fight or take flight, so I play possum and watch the play unfold before me.

Mom doesn't speak for a while, and we all wait with our eyes on her. She sits up straight.

"Well," Mom drags the word out. She shifts her body under the sheets. "I'll think about it. I'm tired right now." When she's finished, she seems deflated. She lies back and presses a button to lower her bed.

Ellyn looks like she's sucking on a sour candy. Peter hunches further.

"Mom, we need to let them know," Peter says, at last finding his voice.

"Yes, Ruth," Ellyn interjects. "They said they'd only hold the place until Tuesday at the latest, so we need a decision from you soon."

"Peter, Ellyn," Mom says, her voice hard like a Marine drill sergeant's. "Don't rush me. I said I need time to think about this."

"All right, Ruth. We'll talk about this later." Ellyn puts on a pair of sunglasses and turns towards Peter. "We better get going."

He nods. "Yeah, okay." Peter crosses the distance from the wall to the side of the bed and kisses our mother on the cheek. "We'll be back tomorrow." He steps back and Ellyn swoops in and kisses Mom.

"I look forward to it," Mom says, her voice gentle. She's pleased. Mom smiles in a benevolent way, indulgent and a little delighted. Peter is still her baby. As they leave the room, she lifts her arm and gives a subdued wave, Queen of England–style.

I whistle as my breath escapes.

Mom shifts towards me, and for a few moments we are like two people in a staring contest. We say nothing. I don't tell her how much I hate her son or what a prick I think he was the other night. I don't tell her how difficult it was to be in the room with them. I don't want to focus on the decades of aggravation in the past. My mom is not yet well, and I'm here to help her.

Angela's Ashes is still on her nightstand, and I pick it up and hold it in my hands. The weight and the smell of paper are a form of comfort.

"How do you like the book, Mom?"

Her head tilts up as a sparkle ignites her blue eyes back to life. "I'm surprised his mother was able to survive losing so many of her children." She shakes her head.

"And I'm surprised *he* survived and was able to write about his horrible childhood." I lean forward, about to say something else about the author's rough childhood, when the squeaky wheels of the lunch cart interrupt us.

A short, stocky woman in cartoon-character scrubs enters with Mom's lunch. I remove things from the overbed table so she has a place to put the tray.

"Thank you." She puts the tray down and pulls the lid off the plate, revealing a turkey sandwich on rye, an anemic pile of limp green beans, and coleslaw. After she's left, Mom picks up half of the sandwich and offers it to me with an outstretched hand.

"No thanks, Mom. You eat. I had a late breakfast."

"Oh, okay." She takes a bite.

Mom was always the slowest eater in our family. When I was a little girl and my dad was still alive, dinner was a race to get to the finish line first. My dad inhaled his food faster than Michael Johnson, the American track and field star, can sprint 200 meters. Peter and I—along with my older half-sister from Dad's first marriage, Liz—would shovel the food in as fast as we could, because whoever was the last one left at the table with Mom had to help wash and dry the dishes. I still eat too fast.

"We haven't talked about it yet but, since Ellyn brought it up, have you given any thought as to where you want to live?"

"I want to go home."

"I know you want to go home, Mom. I wish you could. But Dr. Green said you can't."

I pause for a moment to sort out all my options. Only one seems reasonable. I've watched out for my mother since I was twelve years old, when her husband, my father, died. I'm not certain why I did. Maybe I saw that Peter wasn't there for her. Or maybe I just did what I knew was expected of me as the daughter, a role ingrained in me from birth. This is what the women in our family do. We are the strong ones. We are the ones who take care of our parents when they are old and frail. This is our family culture, and as a daughter I would never abandon my mother, no matter what.

With less thought than I've given to buying a dress, I say, "Would you like to come to the desert?" I don't for a moment believe she will—she's lived in Los Angeles since she was four years old, and in the same zip code for more than fifty years.

"Yes," she says without hesitation.

I'm stunned. I've made no plans for this possibility. Mom has always said she never wants to be a burden on me and would never consider living with me. I guess things change when life goes from a "maybe" in the future to a crisis today. I don't even know if there are any suitable and affordable places in the desert where she can live.

"I want to be close to you. Ellyn and Peter mean well, but I'm not certain they'll remember to take care of me like they said they would. I know I can trust you." Mom's blue eyes penetrate through me like lasers, reading my every thought and emotion. When I was little, I believed Mom knew everything, as though a neon sign printed each thought and action across my forehead.

"You can count on me, Mom."

"I know. You've always been one to do the right thing, even when you were just a small child."

If she only knew all the times I didn't do the right thing—but today's not the day to tell her. Perhaps that day will never come.

⁓

The following Wednesday Mom moves to a rehab facility in Santa Monica, and I head back to the desert to prepare.

PART 2:

INTERREGNUM

. . . .

An interval between two successive reigns, when the country has no sovereign; any break in a series or in a continuity; a lapse or pause in a continuous series

discontinuity, hiatus, hiccup (also hiccough), interim, interlude, intermission, gap, interruption, interstice, interval, parenthesis; interspace

Chapter 6:

Preparation

During periods of discontinuous, abrupt change, the essence of adaptation involves a keen sensitivity to what should be abandoned—not what should be changed or introduced. A willingness to depart from the familiar has distinct survival value.

—Peter F. Drucker

Tonight is my first time at home in ten days. It feels good to be in my own bed with Maggie asleep next to me. It seems a lot longer than just ten days ago that Mom went into the hospital and I rushed to Los Angeles. Seems like a lifetime, and in a way it is, because our lives have changed and will soon change again in ways I cannot imagine when she moves near me.

The room is warm, too warm. The air conditioner is set below seventy, but my bedroom is still uncomfortable. The walls are thin, and heat seeps in behind my head. I throw the covers off my body but leave them over my feet. I don't know why, but I have never felt safe in bed unless my feet are covered.

Tomorrow will be a busy day, and I need to sleep. There's The Mourning Star Center's business to tend to, and I need to find a place close by for Mom to live. There are plenty of assisted care facilities in this area, which is known for taking care of the elderly. I've heard of the desert being called "a place where people come to die."

My first call in the morning is to the executive director of the Joselyn Senior Center, who says there are assisted living apartments right across the street from his facility. He tells me the name and number of the superintendent. I make an appointment for 10:00 a.m., which allows me an hour to return business calls.

Even before I leave my car, I'm certain this place will never work. I gulp past the lump in my throat, force my unwilling body out of the car, and cross the street towards the stale, one-story apartment buildings. Flattop roofs speckled with white gravel sag under the weight of time, as if too tired to hold themselves up for another year. The stucco is an anemic pink-beige. A concrete courtyard in the middle of the apartments is barren except for a battered, round, glass-top table and four worn, uncomfortable-looking strap chairs where a gray-haired lady with dull hazel eyes slumps in a wheelchair. A bald man hunched like Quasimodo shuffles along, his feet scraping the concrete as he walks.

The superintendent, a slender reed of a woman with brassy blonde hair and a cigarette hanging from her thin lips opens the door to show me the one available apartment where we are assaulted by the musty smell of emptiness and age. Dismal curtains, yellowed by years of stagnation, sag at the back of the room and droop towards the worn beige carpet.

"The rent is a mere $2,000 a month, which includes a limited amount of supervision. Tenants are on their own when it comes to meals," she says in a raspy voice.

I can't imagine Mom living in this place that reeks of hopelessness and defeat. Even the bright August sun can't penetrate and breathe a sparkle of life into this end-of-the-line stop. The only positive thing is that it's five minutes from my house and office.

"Okay," I say as I head to the door to make my escape. "There are a few more places I need to check out."

"These apartments go quick," the stick lady says, "so you better decide fast."

"I will. Thank you for your time." I wave without turning to look at her as I scamper away.

The rest of my morning is filled with visits to more drab facilities. With each visit, my spirit sinks further down an emotional ditch. I can only take so much, and head back to my office to catch up on my work and make calls to find out if anyone knows of a nice place to recommend for Mom. I'm desperate. If I don't find a decent residence for her, she'll have to come live with me. Much as I love her, I haven't lived with her since I was twenty, and we didn't get along back then. Although I didn't do it with conscious intention, I believe I married young to escape from her. In 1970, girls only left home to go to college or get married.

It's taken years of therapy and many intense conversations with Mom for us to develop the good relationship we now enjoy. Even so, I'm uneasy with the idea of us living under the same roof.

The next afternoon I visit an assisted care facility called Happy Gardens. The outside murmurs sophistication. The new, tawny

Mediterranean building reminds me of my mother and warm honey milk in a mug on a rare L.A. rainy winter childhood afternoon. The entrance, with its large, wooden French doors under a portico, suggests a high-quality hotel.

I tug open the door to enter a tasteful and inviting lobby filled with colorful upholstered couches and overstuffed chairs around a coffee table in front of a wood-mantled fireplace. To my left, just behind an opening in the wall, sits a dark-haired woman who smiles and greets me with the same warmth a hostess would welcome a guest into her home. When I explain why I'm there, she hands me a clipboard with a questionnaire and a plastic visitor tag on a string necklace to put around my neck.

A few minutes after I return the form, a slender blonde in a stylish, professional gray suit, greets me and introduces herself. She says she's heard good things about my work and the Center I founded. She's warm, kind, and solicitous as she shows me around the facility and points out all the amenities. She feels like a friend.

"As you can tell, we've gone out of our way to select bright, cheery fabrics and colors. We want our guests to feel as though they are staying at a fine hotel." She gestures toward the room.

"Yes, this is lovely. Very homey." My head bobs up and down. "You've done a wonderful job."

She smiles. We pass through a dining room full of tables covered in vibrant pink-and-white tablecloths, and enter a smaller room where there's a party. Well-dressed, gray-haired men and women with cocktails are engaged in conversations, their laughter filling the room. The atmosphere reminds me of the years before Dad died, when my parents' many friends were always at our house drinking, playing poker, and laughing.

I'm about to ask if we're at a private party and must have a quizzical look on my face, because my guide says, "Cocktail hour is every afternoon at four."

"My mom would enjoy this." *Sure she would, but I don't want her to drink.* The idea terrifies me. When my mother drinks she turns into a nightmare. Thank God she stopped drinking in 1987.

———

In 1987, I was in Los Angeles, on my school break staying at The Hilton Hotel next to Robinson's, a high-end department store in Beverly Hills. Mom and I had just finished dinner and come back to my room. I'd given it a lot of thought and knew I needed to talk to her about her drinking or the possibility she had dementia. I had almost completed my first year of graduate school working on my master's in psychology. During a course on alcohol and drug addiction, I realized my mother was an alcoholic. In another class on the psychology of aging, I'd learned there are forms of what we call Alzheimer's that might in reality be a type of senile dementia, which can be halted and reversed if caught soon enough.

During the last year, Mom's behavior had become erratic and unpleasant. Our phone conversations would start out fine, but with no warning I'd be thrown into an emotional pit by her belligerent verbal assaults. I began to call her at 7:00 in the morning because catching her early was my only chance to talk to my safe, reasonable mother. Any later in the day, and a simple conversation would drop into a dungeon where Mom would take even the simplest thing I said and ensnarl it into a distorted pretzel. She'd become defensive and attack me with accusations and criticisms, most of which made no sense. Her words were so bizarre that I couldn't follow what she was saying. I'd attempt to mollify her or clarify what she'd said but that only made her more belligerent. My only escape from her was to say "good-bye" and hang up. Our conversations left me frustrated, scared, and confused.

Now, in this hotel room, with Mom so close, I was terrified the words I was about to say would unleash her venom, but I had to try.

"Mom, I'm extremely concerned about you." I made myself as small and unthreatening as possible, and I could tell that my voice was timid.

"Oh?" She frowned and stared at me, waiting for me to go on.

"Mom, I've noticed some things about your behavior, and either you're in the beginning stages of dementia or you're an alcoholic." I paused for a moment, but she said nothing.

I took a deep breath and continued, "If it's the former, we need to get you to a doctor for a diagnosis, because there are forms of dementia that can be halted when diagnosed early. If it's the latter, then I need to tell you that you either must stop drinking or I can no longer be in relationship with you."

I waited for the assault.

She said nothing, and her expression remained inscrutable. Eons passed. I began to shrink inside like a little child who was in big trouble and was going to get punished. Just as I was starting to think she'd never speak to me again, she shifted in her seat, pursed her lips, and sighed.

"I need to think." She stood up, grabbed her black purse off the bed, and flung the strap over her shoulder.

"I love you, Mom." My voice was high and tense.

"I love you too, Ginni, but I need to leave now." She opened the door and walked out without so much as a glance my way.

For a moment, I didn't move an inch from my spot on the bed. The conversation had ended with no resolution. A minute later, I was flooded with energy and began to pace the room like a trapped tiger, anxious just short of a panic attack. I didn't know what I'd do if she said no. I wondered if I'd have the strength to follow through with my threat, but if I didn't I'd be stuck with Monster Mom, whose words could suck the soul out of my body and wreck a day with no warning.

I jumped at the sudden ring of the phone next to my bed an hour later.

"Ginni, I've been aware for sometime now that my drinking was out of control and how alcohol changed my personality, but if no one noticed, I wasn't going to do anything. I appreciate that you saw me and cared enough to speak to me. I love you very much, and I've decided to stop drinking."

I was relieved and grateful. After we hung up, I pored over her words. In my psychology classes, we were taught that many emotional problems exist because of boundary issues. When Mom said if no one noticed her drinking she wasn't going to do anything, I understood on a deeper level the importance of boundaries. We need to know we are being seen. Even if our behavior is bad, when somebody gives voice to what they see, we are no longer invisible and this lets us know we are loved.

When I returned to school, I told Robin, a classmate who was an expert on alcoholism, about my conversation with my mother. "You don't know how lucky you are," she said. "Most alcoholics choose the alcohol. Your mother must love you a lot."

There are no words to describe what her words meant to me. *My mother loved me. My mother loved me more than alcohol. My mother really loved me.* Okay, maybe I sound like Sally Field's Oscar acceptance speech, but that's how I felt.

I want to hold on to this memory as though it is a lifeline. That was eleven years ago and Mom hasn't had a drink since that time, and our relationship became a deep, fun, intimate friendship. My mother loves me but will she be able to resist the temptation of alcohol if she moves into Happy Gardens?

———

After the blonde lady has shown me all the available rooms, we tour the rest of the facility, which includes an ice cream parlor, hair salon, gym, library, and a special movie room. When we return to her office, she perches in a large chair behind a bulky wood desk that dwarfs her. I sit across from her in a small, hard, metal chair and listen while she goes over the costs of the rooms. The least expensive is $3,500, and the price will rise as Mom requires more and more care.

She's been so pleasant the whole time we've been together, and because she knows the work I do in the community, I believe I can talk to her like a friend.

"$3,500 is more than we can afford. Can you do any better than that?"

The words barely escape my lips when her face falls like she's had a sudden attack of Bell's palsy. Her mask of kindness melts away. She bolts out of her chair, races over to me, and yanks the visitor pass off my neck.

I stand up with every intention of telling her what I think about her behavior, but my mouth opens and no words come out. I'm frozen and wordless, which is typical when someone is mean to me. If I try to speak I know I'll cry, and there is no way I'll let her see me cry. My reaction is one of three ways any animal—and we humans *are* animals—reacts when threatened. We either fight, flee, or freeze. Peter trained me to freeze long ago. If I fought back or ran when he threatened me, he'd hit me harder.

The first time he did this after Dad died, he left a handprint on my thigh that stayed there for more than a week. After many decades of therapy, my reaction to meanies is still the same: I freeze. "You shouldn't have come here if you couldn't afford it. You might want to consider an inexpensive nursing home." She stomps over to the door in a rush, opens it, and shoves me through. The door slams behind me.

I didn't do anything wrong, but I am mortified, like a chastised child. I slump back to my car with my head down and start the engine to let the air conditioner cool the car. I sit behind the wheel, too upset to drive. My body shakes and my face is hot. I close my eyes and focus on my breath until I'm calm enough to ease the car into gear.

As soon as I'm home, I search the Internet and write a scathing letter to the president of the corporation on my Center's letterhead and sign it as the executive director. I want to make sure this blonde woman never humiliates anyone again.

My mood doesn't improve. I can't shake this blanket of shame, which is a lot more than I need to wear on this hot night. I want to run from the hurt child buried inside me who rises with a force and captures my emotions whenever I feel threatened or hurt by someone. Jung would say I'd dropped into a complex, a place inside us that develops at a young age. Once we're in it, everything we see and hear is colored by this emotional space.

I can't indulge in this right now. There's a lot to do before Mom is released from rehab. I've come to the conclusion after a week of looking at every available facility that I no longer have a choice: Mom has to live with me.

I've run out of time and options, so the next step is to get my house ready. The following morning I shop for items necessary to make my home safe and comfortable. First stop, a store in Cathedral City called Yes I Can where I find grab bars, the name of a handyman to install them, a commode to place over the toilet or use in her room if the time comes when Mom can no longer walk to the bathroom, and an alert system for Mom to wear around her neck or keep at her bedside to let me know if she's in any trouble via its other component, which I'll keep in my bedroom.

While she's been in rehab, I've driven to Santa Monica twice a week to visit Mom. The rehab facility reminds me of a gray, dour, square institution of a building out of Jane Eyre. Mom shares a long, stark, clean room with three other women. Her bed is closest to the door, and she looks up from her book and smiles when I enter. Over the weeks, the severe bruises on her arms have mottled into blurred red, blue, and yellow blotches.

She's been there for two weeks, and the doctor says she'll be able to go home in a few days. We discuss what she wants from her apartment. A male friend with a van has come with me to help out. She doesn't want much: her teacup collection, her mother's china, her maple drop front desk, her toiletries, clothes, TV set, and, to my surprise, the book *Tuesdays with Morrie*. She says she doesn't care about the rest of her things, but I wonder if she finds it that simple to let go of a lifetime of things she's gathered and the memories attached to them.

⁓

Dark shadows cast a deep sadness across Mom's apartment. The living room is filled with furniture she purchased in 1963. The round dining room table and green chairs she's had since soon after Dad died remind me of that other time in my life when everything changed in an instant. Her blue-and-white couch sags in front of two tall oak bookcases that straddle an oblong window with a view of large apartment buildings, rooftops, and the smoggy L.A. sky.

I move around like a detective and scan the apartment for some of my special favorites. The antique waffle iron and small iron with the inner space to fill with hot coals, which were part of a collection of antiques from our backyard, and a small wood cabinet that used to be in our living room are nowhere in sight.

I find many photographs of Peter and Ellyn atop every piece of furniture in her living room, but I don't see myself anywhere. In her bedroom, a large black-and-white photograph of a cute, curly light-haired, four-year-old Peter stands on one end of her maple dresser, where it's resided for as long as I can recall. At the other end, a small, painted photograph of me, taken when I was five, rests in a small, tarnished, oval gold frame with pink matting. Next to that is a tiny color photograph of my ex-husband and me taken in 1982. The photographs in the bedroom are the only ones I pack.

Peter is supposed to come later to take care of the furniture. The day in the hospital a few weeks ago will turn out to be the last time we see each other.

Chapter 7:

Home Invasion

*Any idiot can face a crisis; it's this day-to-day living that
wears you out . . .*

—Anton Chekov

SUNDAY, AUGUST 1, 1999

If this were a screenplay for a movie, the opening would read
like this:

EXT. FLAT-ROOF CREAM-COLOR
HOUSE—DAY

Threatening Witch music from The Wizard of Oz. *Da da–da da
–da da da.*

But this isn't a movie. This is my life, and there is no soundtrack
or theme music.

"It's too hot," Mom grumbles as she gets out of my car and hurries to the front door.

"I know, Mom. That's summer in the desert."

"Yuck."

I open the door and step aside to allow Mom to enter first. She skulks past me into my home, now her home, with a scowl. Maggie strolls over to us with a big white Flossie, a toy that doubles as doggie dental floss, in her mouth, tail wagging. Mom smiles and pats Maggie on her head. After I say hello and scratch her favorite spot on her back near her tail, Maggie saunters away from us and plops down on the cool tile floor in the kitchen.

I escort Mom to her new bedroom and point out the canisters I've had installed in the ceiling over the head of the queen-size bed so she'll have plenty of light when she reads.

"I had the cable company come out and your TV is all hooked up and ready to go."

She nods and walks over to the window to the left of the dresser where the TV sits, and looks out through the open shutter slats. "The trees are pretty," she says.

"Yes. We have Meyer lemon, tangelo, pink grapefruit, orange, and peach trees. The peaches are already gone and the grapefruit, orange, and tangelo will ripen in the fall."

"I've never heard of a Meyer lemon."

"Oh, it's the best lemon you've ever had. The rind is thinner and the juice much sweeter than the normal lemon. I always keep Meyer lemon ice cubes in the freezer so you can put them in a glass of water."

"You know I don't drink water." Her face puckers as she sticks out her tongue and she shakes her head.

"Well, you're going to have to now that you're living in the desert."

"I don't have to do anything." She turns away from me and doesn't see my fist glued to my scrunched mouth. The carpet mutes the impatient sound of my foot tapping against the floor.

I want to tell her how crucial water is in the desert, but I'm certain she won't listen to me. Time to move on.

"Let me show you the bathrooms you'll be using."

I lead her through the doorway to the right of her wicker bed into the bathroom connected to her new bedroom, one of the two bathrooms she'll use. The bathroom consists of two rooms; the one we're in has a brown-tiled counter with a white farmer's sink and is next to a smaller room with a toilet and bathtub/shower combination with the same brown tile. I open the drawers to show Mom where I've placed her toiletries.

"Thank you," Mom nods and moves towards the room with the toilet. She stops at the door, and her body stiffens. "What's that?" She points to the seat with handles above the toilet.

"That's a commode. It has bars to hold onto, and the higher seat will make it easier for you to sit because you won't need to bend down so far." Her eyes narrow when I add, "It comes with a bucket, and if you're ever too sick, we can bring this into your room so that you can use the toilet without having to walk as far."

Only after the words escape from my mouth do I realize this is too much information. I've never been good at knowing when to quit talking while I was ahead, and I'm certain the sight of the commode had me behind before I opened my mouth. Yep, I lost her at "commode."

I rush her out of the room and escort her down the hall to the other bathroom. "Mom, I got you grab bars to hold onto. I bought the best ones I could find." I point to the decorative bar outside the shower. "I decided this should be the room where you bathe because these couldn't be installed in the other bathroom without making it awkward for you to get into the shower."

I open the shower door and show her the other grab bar, the extra-safe non-slip mat, bathing chair, and special handheld showerhead I bought for her. I watch her like an expectant child, but I'm rewarded with a frown and a grunt.

I lead her back to her bedroom, where I'm sure she'll be happier with the other things I got her.

Mom walks over to the dresser and her eyes rest on her black inlaid onyx set consisting of a large handheld mirror; a cracked, smaller mirror with a bendable handle; and a small, lidded, round jar. She fondles each piece with a wistful smile. She's had this set for as long as I can remember. I have no idea when she bought them or if they were a gift. I don't know why I never asked.

She turns back toward me. "Where'd you put my jewelry case?"

"In the top drawer."

She opens the drawer and picks up a weathered, oval, leather case and rubs her fingers over the abstract, raised pattern carved into the tan surface. She holds it with the same gentleness a mother holds her baby.

"My mother gave this to me," she says. "She'd been in the hospital for months and she was dying and somehow she got this for me. I don't know how she did it. This is the only thing I remember her ever giving me." She shakes her head ever so slightly and with a wistful sigh returns the case to the drawer.

"That's so special, Mom."

"She was special. My mother was the smartest person I've ever known."

"Including me, Mom?" I say with a playful smile.

"No. Of course not. You're brilliant."

I don't let her words inside where they might soothe me. Why do her harsh words penetrate and stick while her praise echoes off into the distance?

"I have more things for you, Mom." I point towards the glass nightstand at the left of her bed.

Mom picks up and begins to fiddle with the alarm system I got her, a small white square on a white string. "What is this?"

"An alarm system you wear around your neck so that if something happens and you need me, all you do is push the little button and I'll be alerted to come help you."

"Oh," she says as frost begins to cover everything in the room. You've never lived until you've heard one of my mother's "ohs." That small, two-letter word speaks volumes, but the tune is anything but melodic. No one can chop a word into shards like my mom. I'm certain she doesn't realize how she slices into me when she does this.

Although I'm hurt, I'm not ready to give up.

"I got you something special, Mom." I hold a small, gift-wrapped box in my outstretched hand.

Mom hesitates but doesn't look at me before she takes the box.

"Open it, Mom. I think you'll like it."

I'm certain she'll love the pretty, pink leather Raika calendar and address book. I scouted everything at The Village Inscriber, an upscale stationery store in my neighborhood, before I purchased this expensive gift for Mom. I'd never buy anything this pricey for myself, but after all Mom has been through I wanted to give her a gift that would make her feel special.

She opens the box, pulls back the tissue, and stares at her gift for a moment before removing it. No smile.

"Do you like it?" My neck cranes forward and my eyes are wide with expectation.

I want her to toss me something, but she just looks at it and when she does speak, her "yes" is as dry as the harsh desert outside.

I swallow hard.

I can't believe how excited I was to show Mom everything I did for her. I want her to be comfortable and happy here, but so far she hasn't liked anything I've done. I slink inside myself and try to shove down the rush of emotions rumbling inside, but they're too strong. I wish I didn't feel so unsettled by her presence and ruffled by my feelings of failure. I never stop to consider what this massive disruption to her life means to my mother, or that she has just faced down her own death. I fail to consider her vulnerability or how afraid she might be. I don't know if she is aware of those things in herself, or if this is her experience, because I don't ask. We seem to be isolated, blind women lost in this new life, and we continue to bump against one another. Our relationship reminds me of "All I Know," the Jimmy Webb song performed by Simon & Garfunkel, which speaks of the way two people can easily bruise each other despite knowing at a deeper level that their love is the only thing of importance.

And so, although the physical space between us is smaller than it has been for almost thirty years, the emotional space is our own Grand Canyon, deep, wide, and treacherous.

"I'm extremely tired, Ginni. I'm going to lie down and take a nap."

"Okay. You must be exhausted after all you've been through." I kiss her on the cheek before I make my escape.

I race across the house towards my bedroom. Maggie follows and scoots in before I shut the door. I can't scream or swear
because I no longer live alone and Mom might hear me, so I am
in a silent fury as I pace back and forth across the room, shaking,
my insides on fire.

This is the first day, the first hour. What have I gotten myself into?

Chapter 8:

First Week

Problems are not the problem; coping is the problem.

—Virginia Satir

MONDAY

Mom is in my kitchen. I'm grateful she's already made coffee. One less thing my sleep-deprived, foggy mind has to accomplish first thing in the morning. I let Maggie outside and retrieve the newspaper, which Mom grabs and begins to scan as she settles into a chair at the kitchen desk. Mom's a reader, whether it's a newspaper, magazine, or book. She always reads and will until the end of her life.

The illness and move away from all her friends has left Mom with few pleasures. Reading is the most reliable and the one thing that has been with her since she was a small child. She's told me stories about her early life—she was born in Montreal, Canada in 1914 and came to the United States with her mother to Vermont when she was seven months old. When she was four, they moved to Los Angeles and lived in an area called Leimert Park. From the time she was no more than five years old, she would go to the library and check out a stack of books. She'd read them as she walked and would often finish all the books before she got home. She's always devoured books and my childhood home was filled with them. Everyone in the house read, but the one I remember most is Mom. She is the one who read to me. I would curl into her arms and listen to the rise and fall of her voice as she performed the words on the page. Mom bequeathed to me the love of books and a fierce curiosity to learn.

Mom and I don't say much to each other this first morning in the kitchen. We are early risers but not early socializers, so a quick hello and retreat to my room is fine with both of us.

A couple of hours later, we meet back in the kitchen to go shopping. Mom needs the right shoes and clothes to survive the searing desert heat. She wears a polyester black-and-white blouse, white pants, and black leather shoes. Her feet are swollen, red, and puff above her flats like freshly baked bread.

"We need to get you some sandals, Mom."

"I hate sandals. Never wear them."

"I know you don't, but look at your feet."

She looks down and then up at me, a question on her face as though she hadn't seen the obvious.

"I got you this to help keep you cool," I say and hand her a pink plastic bottle. "You move this black switch to the right and it turns on the fan. Squeeze the bottle and water is forced through the fan to cool you off." She glances at the bottle and with great alacrity places it on the counter, as though she can't get rid of the unpleasant object fast enough.

I take her to SAS Shoes and get her to try on a pair of sandals. I put a pair on to prove they aren't so bad. I saunter past her like a model, cooing about how cushy, comfortable, and cute they are.

"You should have been an actress," Mom says with a smile.

Whatever I did works, because she allows me to buy her two pairs, a black and a beige. She tries to stuff her foot back into her leather shoe but can't get it in and is forced to wear the black sandals out of the store, which no doubt gives her poor feet a reprieve.

The next stop is a dress shop for some casual summer dresses.

"I don't want this. It has no shape." She wrinkles her nose at the blue shift I've pulled off the rack.

"I know, Mom, but trust me, it's hot right now and it's going to get hotter, and the less fabric hugging your body the more comfortable you'll be."

I buy her three colorful dresses. The pink and blue ones are floor-length and sleeveless, and a third dress is black with cap sleeves and flares out just below her knees.

Mom doesn't thank me for the clothes, but I still want to do something to make her happy, so I say, "How about lunch, Mom?"

She shakes her head and her body droops a little. "I'm too tired. I can't stand this heat. I want to go home."

Our drive home is silent. When we get there, I prepare a sandwich for her before I head to my office to pick up the mail. I leave her seated at the kitchen desk, paperback book in hand, so engrossed I'm not sure she hears me say I'm leaving. She doesn't stir when I kiss her and say good-bye.

When I return, I find her in the family room watching TV, the other thing Mom has always done, at least since Dad died. I don't think either of them watched much while he was alive because they were too busy partying with friends or playing cards. After he died, Mom's life narrowed down to not much more than work, then coming home to drink and prepare dinner, eat, and head for the den. She'd settle into her favorite ivory chair with her cigarettes and Scotch and spend the rest of the night in front of the TV. She'd only get up to pour another drink or change the channel.

I'm grateful that she no longer smokes or drinks.

THURSDAY

I take Mom for an appointment with my doctor. She's still on Coumadin and has to be watched closely. I'm relieved she likes him and grateful he agreed to bring her into his busy practice. He's the only doctor I know who still does blood tests in his office, so I won't need to drag her someplace else.

Our next stop is my hairdresser, who gives Mom an updated haircut and style. Mom looks better than she has in years. She knows it, too. She struts off the chair and strides out of the salon with her shoulders back and her head high.

As soon as we're both in the car and I've started the engine, Mom says, "I want to get you something for your fiftieth birthday. What do you want?"

I think about it a minute, then turn toward Mom. "I'd like something that can't wear out; something I'll always have."

"Jewelry?"

"Yes, I think so."

I've never bought jewelry since I've been living in the desert and don't know where the jewelry stores are, so I drive a few blocks down El Paseo, a street called "The Rodeo Drive of the desert." I stop at a store with a big "sale" sign in the window.

Behind the glass counter, a large woman with tousled, short blonde hair greets us with enthusiasm. "Welcome. What can I do for you?"

Mom tells her she wants to buy a present for my fiftieth birthday, and the lady takes us over to a counter with sale items. "Do you like that one?" Mom asks as she points to a gold band with a cabochon ruby in the center surrounded by three small diamonds on each side.

"I do." I'm surprised and delighted she's selected something this nice.

I'm even more pleased to find that it fits.

"We'll take it," Mom says.

"Fantastic," the blonde lady says. "Now, if you also buy the duplicate cabochon emerald ring, I'll give both of them to you for just one hundred dollars more."

I don't think Mom can afford that, but before I can voice my dissent Mom chimes in, "You like them, honey, they're yours. We'll take them."

"Thank you, Mom." I bend down to hug her and kiss her on the cheek, and I can tell by her smile that she's pleased.

"It's wonderful to see a mother and daughter who love each other so much and get along so well," the blonde lady says. "Max, Rachel, come here," she calls out. "You've got to see this. This woman just bought her daughter two rings for her birthday. They are so sweet."

I hold out my hand and Max and Rachel cluck with appreciation. "You're a wonderful mother," they say. Mom stands taller.

"You two must have the best relationship."

"We do." I know I'm a fraud. We're frauds. Mom and I haven't gotten along since she moved in, and while I'm certain one day I will be glad to have these rings, right now they can't heal the hurt and disappointment of the last few days.

Next stop, lunch at Sammy's Woodfired Pizza on the upper floor of The Gardens on El Paseo, an outdoor mall completed not long ago. We slide into the peach booth and the waitress hands us each a menu, which Mom pores over like a student preparing for a test.

"What can I get you," the waitress says after returning with two glasses of water.

"I'll have the angel hair pasta with shrimp and an iced tea," Mom says without looking at the waitress.

"I'll have the chopped chicken salad with olives." I smile up at the waitress as I hand her our menus. She turns to walk away when I call out, "Oh, and for dessert, bring us a Messy Sundae."

"What's that?" Mom asks.

"Just wait, Mom, you're going to looove this," I say with a Cheshire cat grin.

After we finish the main course, the waitress places our dessert in the middle of the table and gives both of us long spoons.

"You're in for a treat, Mom."

"Oh, boy!" Mom smiles as she dips her long silver spoon through the maraschino cherry–topped ruffled mountain of whipped cream and down into the mixture of vanilla ice cream covered with chocolate and caramel syrups sprinkled with walnuts. The chocolate drips all the way down the sides of the tall, stemmed glass and puddles in a dark brown oasis at the bottom of the plate. I don't hesitate; I take a big scoop from my side. The coolness of the ice cream mixed with the chocolate soothes and smooths away the anxiety that's been inside me since Mom arrived.

Chocolate brings us together. Mom and I have always loved

chocolate. We didn't have many sweets in our house growing up, but Mom always had a bar of chocolate hidden somewhere in the house and each evening she'd break off a piece. I wasn't allowed to have any because I had bad teeth and the doctor said I couldn't eat sweets. But once a year, on my birthday, I got to have cake and it was always chocolate. In the late 1970s, I went to Ghirardelli Square in San Francisco with my boyfriend, and because he adored my mom, he bought her a five-pound bar of chocolate. She was beyond thrilled when she saw it. A month later she kidded that she'd never be able to eat another piece of chocolate again. That declaration didn't last because her passion for chocolate was too strong to restrain.

Although Mom and I connect over this shared love, it's more of a temporary truce than a true end of all conflict.

I guess most mother-daughter relationships are conflicted. We can argue, be mad, think terrible thoughts one moment, and in the next, all is forgotten and forgiven, and we're the best of friends.

My shoulders relax and fall away from my ears as a chink of emotional armor comes off. Today was the first easy day since she moved in. Maybe we've outrun the storm and are in for clear sailing.

If only it were that simple.

Chapter 9:

Freedom

Freedom lies in being bold.
—Robert Frost

SEPTEMBER

The day comes when I watch Mom cross the circular driveway, get into her silver Thunderbird and drive off.

"Ginni, I miss playing bridge and want to get started again. I've called around and there's a game this afternoon."

"Are you sure you're up to it?" I'm trying to be patient but I know I'm frowning at her. "Okay, Mom. Where do I take you?"

"I'll drive myself," she says, looking determined.

"Are you sure?" She looks healthy and strong to me, but I'm not a medical doctor. I never thought she'd drive again, but Mom has always been one resilient and determined lady.

"Yes. I'm ready. I can't have you stopping your life for me. It isn't fair." This is the first crumb of a thought about my welfare she's tossed my way since she's been here.

I go to her side and as I lean down to put my arms around her, she reaches up, and we embrace in a deep, though quick, hug. Mom's never been very demonstrative, at least with me. She says I'm not affectionate and doesn't hug me because when I was a baby I pushed her away. She was demonstrative with Dad and somehow that piece of her died when he did.

⌒

I recall a time when I was eleven years old and we'd driven with Dad to San Pedro, where his boat was docked. I was in the middle of the bench seat between Mom and Dad, my usual spot when the three of us were in the car.

"Good-bye, Ginni," Dad said as he gave me a kiss on the cheek.

"Good-bye, Daddy." I kissed him back.

Then I saw something so icky, my stomach began to tighten in disgust. Dad and Mom reached across me and melded into each other's arms, complete with a big, open-mouth kiss. I'd never seen them chew on each other's faces before. In 1960, movie kisses were closed-mouth, not like now, when the audience gets to be a voyeur, so I'd never witnessed this type of affection. I knew I'd never do anything so gross.

Mom only had two dates after Dad died, and I don't know if either of them ended with a kiss. Perhaps the passionate side of her life ended thirty-eight long years ago and she forgot or lost all her ability for strong emotions. Much of the woman she was and mother I knew was lost and buried with my father when I was still a child.

After our embrace, I return to the kitchen counter, take my last sip of coffee, and fling the rest into the sink.

"I'm off," Mom says. Her purse hangs from the crook of her arm, her keys dangling. Looking out the kitchen window, I watch her drive away in her 1989 silver Thunderbird, feeling, I imagine, as a parent does the first time a teenage child gets a driver's license and leaves home alone. I'm not as certain as Mom is about her ability to drive, but know I must let her do this if she's ever going to reclaim her life.

Her freedom is my freedom.

Chapter 10:

No Time To Say Good-Bye

Grief is so painfully real, regardless of its origin. The love of, and attachment to, an animal friend can equal that of human relationships. Likewise, the loss of an animal can be just as devastating.

—Rev. Joel L. Morgan

Anyone with a heart . . . has experienced loss. No one escapes unscathed. Every story of separation is different, but I think we all understand that basic, wrenching emotion that comes from saying goodbye…

—Luanne Rice

THURSDAY, OCTOBER 21, 1999

I loved Maggie the moment I held her in my arms and inhaled her sweet breath. She made soft *uh-uh-uh* puppy sounds, and a smile opened in my grieving heart. I peered into her golden eyes and said, "I know how this ends, and I'm only willing to do this again because I loved Holly so much." Holly, my sixteen-and-a-half-year-old, thirty-five-pound, red, brown, and black mixture of a magical dog, died in my arms on February 4, 1988. On May 28, a sunny, warm spring afternoon, I enfolded this darling Golden Retriever puppy, a yellow fluff of blonde hair, into my arms for the first time. *Maggie* was whispered to me, and I was certain this was her name.

The subsequent eleven and a half years raced by, punctuated with the sudden death of my beautiful black-and-white German Shepherd, Samantha; the end of my twelve-year marriage; a 500-mile move southeast to the desert; a serious car accident; my mother coming to live with me; and now this, the night of October 21, 1999, when death slips into my house and at 7:45 p.m. steals my Maggie.

———

A few weeks ago, a routine blood test showed something wrong. Nancy, her vet, said they didn't think it was any big deal but wanted to schedule an ultrasound to make sure. We had to wait almost two weeks for the man with the ultrasound equipment to come to her office.

This morning Nancy assured me she was certain the worst thing they'd find was a problem with Maggie's spleen, which would require only minor surgery, and she'd be good as new. I believed her so I didn't worry.

We're at Nancy's office now, in the large, white, sterile, cold, L-shaped waiting room. Lysol-masked urine assaults my lungs. Maggie lies next to my feet. Her head is up, her curious amber eyes scan the room, and her breathing is her normal *I'm-at-the-vet's* pant.

When the tech comes, Maggie doesn't look back as she's led

away. I ignore the catch in my throat and decide I'm not too concerned, because they'll either find nothing or only the simple spleen issue Nancy told me about. I don't like the idea of Maggie needing surgery, but I'm certain she'll be okay. Death never joins my chorus of thoughts.

I try to read my book but I can't keep track of the words, so I wait and fidget while I stare at the door. After about twenty long minutes, Nancy, a pretty, petite, blonde woman in her early forties, enters the room and marches towards me—without Maggie. I am alarmed by her grave expression, but before I can speak, she tells me to come with her and points towards a door on the left I'd never noticed.

Nancy opens the door, enters, and flips on the fluorescent light, revealing a windowless gray room furnished with a steel desk and two stiff black chairs.

"Sit down." She gestures to one of the chairs. Nancy pulls the other chair right up to me so we're sitting knee-to-knee. She leans forward and touches my leg, her serious brown eyes staring into mine.

"I'm sorry to tell you this." Her voice is deep, with no hint of her usual mirth. She hesitates as though she's weighing her words.

Every muscle in my body stiffens.

"Maggie has pancreatic cancer and only four days to live."

I bow my head, shaken—then, strengthened by a deep breath, I look at Nancy. The soft concern in her expression rips into me, and I struggle to hold back bitter tears. I try to sit straight with resolve.

"Four days?" I ask, hoping she'll change her story.

"I'm so sorry." She scribbles something on a scrap of paper and hands it to me. "This is my cell phone number. Call me any time. Any time." I take the number from her and shove it into my purse.

"You can stay in my office as long as you like. Use my phone if there's anyone you want to call. Joanne will bring Maggie to you in a few minutes."

"Thank you," I murmur, sounding like the sad child that I am.

When she leaves I call my friend Eileen, the one person in the desert who loves Maggie almost as much as I do. I pace the room, twisting the phone cord, while I wait for her to answer. The sound of her voice offers some comfort but not enough to stop the stabs to my heart. My girl, my puppy, is going to die, and no soft words can change that.

Joanne opens the door, releases the leash, and my strawberry blonde, tail-wagging Maggie strolls over to my side. Joanne hovers at the doorway for a moment, glances at me, but says nothing before she disappears. I bend down to Maggie and pet her with soft long strokes. I kiss the top of her head but stop short of making a fuss. With every ounce of determination I can muster, I will away my tears.

When we get home, Maggie walks into the house ahead of me and scampers over to my mother, who sits at the desk area in the kitchen. Mom pets her and turns towards me.

"Well?" She seems soft and gentle. It's the voice of the mother who took wonderful care of me when I was a little girl.

"She's got pancreatic cancer. Her vet says she has four days to live." My voice is flat. I stay away from the emotional truth of my stark words.

"Four days?" Mom's blue eyes darken and she shakes her head. She pets Maggie for another moment, then turns her attention back to her dinner and her paperback book.

Maggie walks to the other side of the kitchen and lays down in her usual position next to the center island. She lies on her stomach with her pretty head up, panting just like always.

Mom gets up and rinses her dish. Without another glance Maggie's way, she goes into the family room, sits down, and turns on the TV. The volume seems louder than normal. She focuses on Wheel of Fortune, oblivious to Maggie and me only a few steps away.

I bend down to Maggie and stroke her gently. She doesn't move. Her head is flat on the floor. Her breathing has changed and deepened into slow, rhythmic ins and outs. I lie down on the floor next to her, coo her name, and continue to pet her. Her eyes are open but she doesn't respond. Her gaze is far off, and if she's aware of me, she shows no sign. I've seen this stare on the hospice ward, but here in my kitchen I don't want to acknowledge that death is in the room. Maggie is supposed to live four more days. I demand every second of those four days, and a miracle extension.

I rub her head, saying, "I'll be right back, girl." I retrieve the piece of paper with Nancy's cell phone number from my purse, but when I dial her number, I get a recording.

Where is she? She said I could call her any time if I needed her. Shit! It's only been a half hour. Why did she give me her phone number with the assurance she'd be there if she wasn't going to be? I'd be pissed but I'm too scared and concerned about what's happening to Maggie to allow these thoughts to take up residence. I leave a message telling her what I've observed and ask her to call me back right away.

I squat down to massage Maggie's laboring body. I put my head next to hers and whisper, "Maggie, I'm here." Her eyes don't refocus.

I don't know what to do, so I call Eileen, who gives me the number of an after-hours vet.

I dial the number and after I explain Maggie's diagnosis and what I'm seeing, the gentle female voice tells me to take Maggie's temperature while she waits.

"It's 105."

"That's high. You better bring her in right away."

After we hang up I call Eileen. She sounds busy but when I explain what's going on and that I need help lifting Maggie so I can take her to the emergency vet, Eileen sighs and says she'll be right over.

I return to Maggie and lay on the floor with her. Her breaths are deep and intermittent. The dings and applause from the TV seem to grow louder. I try to push the sound out of my mind and focus only on Maggie, but the noise is like a bulldozer that heaves me over an emotional cliff.

"Mom! I think Maggie is dying. Please stop the TV."

She squints at me for a brief moment then looks back at the TV and turns the sound down.

"MOM! PLEASE! Turn off the damn TV!" I say with a sharpness I regret. I sound like my mother did when she'd bellow from her bedroom, "Keep it down!" while my friends and I played in my room. I hated that when I was eight, and I hate it now when I hear it in my own voice.

Mom starts to say something, but instead turns off the TV and leaves the room.

Maggie and I are alone. I wish I were strong enough to pick her up and carry her to the car.

After what seems like hours beyond an eternity, the doorbell rings. I rush to open the front door. Eileen, a petite woman with short gray hair, enters. I lead her to the kitchen.

Eileen bends down to Maggie and strokes her head, but she doesn't respond. Eileen looks up at me, a question in her large blue eyes.

My tear-filled eyes are my only answer.

"Ginni, I don't think we should try to take her to the vet's."

"I think you're right." My voice is a choked whisper.

Within minutes, while Eileen and I caress her and talk to her, Maggie exhales a deep breath and never takes another. Eileen and I stare at each other and our eyes convey the words that neither of us can speak.

"She waited for you, Eileen. She loved you." I cave in a little, starting to cry. Eileen's eyes are deep, reflective pools of my own pain. I'm certain my heart has cracked into pieces.

We continue to pet Maggie.

Eileen suggests we put Maggie on a towel and move her into the next room. I get a towel, and we scoot Maggie's body onto it. Maggie looks like she's asleep except there's no movement in her chest.

Mom, now in her pajamas, comes out of her bedroom and looks at me with a quizzical expression.

"Maggie's dead," I whisper.

Mom stops moving. "Oh." She shakes her head then disappears into her bedroom. I understand why she doesn't come closer. Years ago, she told me that she could care for her mother and first husband while they were sick, but once she knew they were dead she could no longer touch them or go near their bodies. Same thing with my Dad; once she was told he was dead, she got up and left his body to the care of others.

As Eileen and I continue to stroke Maggie, I feel the energy leave different points of her body. After about an hour, the last bit of her life force streams from her belly and moves past us and towards the window like a mild breeze. I've seen this before in my work, and understand that although a body dies, our energy, or what some call the soul, continues on.

We continue to rub Maggie for a few moments, then Eileen tells me she has to get home. I escort her to the front door and say good-bye with a grateful hug.

Almost as soon as I've closed the door behind her, the phone rings.

"Hi, it's Nancy. Listen, there's nothing to worry about. It's natural that she'd be breathing like that due to the medication I gave her . . ."

I cut her off before she can continue. "Maggie's dead. She died about an hour ago."

"You don't realize how lucky you are. The next four days would have been really ugly. You're lucky she went so fast."

Lucky! I don't think I'm lucky, although I know what Nancy means. Maggie's death could have been long, painful, drawn out torture for both of us. She went fast and never seemed to be in any pain. While I understand what she means, I don't feel blessed. The only thing important to me is that my wonderful, beautiful Maggie, so full of life less than two hours ago, is gone, and all I'm left with is the sucky pain of grief. If this is luck, I don't want any part of it.

"I'll send my assistants over tomorrow to pick her up. You want her cremated, right?"

"Yes, please."

———

The next morning I shuffle into the kitchen towards the coffee maker next to the sink. I don't want to glance toward Maggie lying in the next room, because if I see her my nightmare will be real. But like the lookie-loos on the freeway, I can't stop myself and I turn my head. Her lifeless body is where I left her last night. I bend down to be close and stroke her cold body, whispering words of love. I wish my love could breathe life back into her, and like a child's magical thinking, I watch her and wait for her to wake up. I continue to pet her until the pain of touching her lifeless shell hurts more than I can tolerate.

I return to the kitchen and pour myself a cup of coffee, sipping while I gaze out the window at the brown Santa Rosa Mountains across the street.

"You're lucky it wasn't me." Mom's voice invades my reverie and I flinch. I put my cup down.

I don't turn around. I can't because the rage inside me is so intense that if I do, I won't be able to stop venomous words escaping from my mouth. I brace myself, hands flat on the white tile counter, and glare at the mountains. I want to yell, "Lucky? Maggie would never say such a thing!" Instead, I remain quiet.

My emotions are out of proportion to her words, but this isn't the first time I've heard them. Mom said the same thing many times in the years after my father died. I missed my dad and hated when she'd say this. I didn't feel lucky then and I don't feel lucky now.

A knock on the door comes just in time to prevent a fight.

"It must be the techs from the vet's office," I say as I head towards the front door. I open the door, and a young man and woman wearing scrubs introduce themselves and offer their condolences. I thank them and lead them to Maggie. They let me cut a locket of her hair and hand me her collar before they pick her up with gentle care and carry her out the door.

And now Mom and I are alone.

Chapter 11:

Crossing the Abyss

We have our problems and we stick together to deal with them.

—Debbie Reynolds

Maggie has been dead a few days and I am so angry with Mom I could spit. Why is she so insensitive? How could she watch TV while Maggie struggled for one more breath? And what in the world would make her say I'm lucky it wasn't her while my dog lay dead in the next room? She said the exact same thing after my dad died. She annoys the hell out of me.

She is awful, and poor me is stuck with her.

I could hold on to that idea but, hard as it is to admit, there's more to the story, more than I realize. I will do my best to guess how it was for her, based on what she's told me.

My mother has had her share of death. Her mother, Goldie, died in 1939 at age fifty-two when Mom was twenty-five years old. Goldie spent the last six months of her life in the hospital, fighting the non-Hodgkin's Disease that was ruthlessly stealing her young life. Mom told me Goldie was afraid and called her every day, the conversations always the same:

"Rutie," Goldie would say, her thick Lithuanian accent cutting each word despite almost a quarter of a century in America, "you must come. I'm dying."

Mom would drop everything, sometimes the curling iron she used to style a customer's hair into a Marcel wave, and run to her mother's side. One day Goldie handed Mom a tissue-wrapped gift—"the only present she ever gave me," she told me. Inside was a tooled leather jewelry case embossed with light swirls surrounding three raised black rectangles. How Goldie was able to purchase this gift for her daughter while in the hospital remains a mystery. Goldie's death created an empty ache my mother carried with her the rest of her life.

While Goldie lay dying, Mom learned her husband Jimmy had nephritis and only ten years to live. She was twenty-four years old and Jimmy was twenty-five. At first the doctor told Mom not to tell Jimmy, and she kept the secret until they realized he had to know because he wasn't taking good care of himself. Four years later, Mom gave birth to Peter. Jimmy lived only eight of the promised ten years and died three months before Peter reached his fourth birthday.

In the late 1970s, Peter's ex-wife Rachel told me that he hit me because he never forgave Mom for getting pregnant when she knew Jimmy was dying.

"That's why he hit me? I had nothing to do with it."

"He said he hit you because he couldn't hit his mother and because he felt guilty about molesting you when you were a little girl."

I would have appreciated a simple *I'm sorry* from Peter a lot more than what I got.

Mom never told me how long Jimmy was in the hospital before he died. She said he was in a coma and when he came out of it, he said, "I heard them talking about someone who's dying. Who's dying?" Those words sent my mother out into the hallway to chastise the nurses and other staff members. In 1946, they didn't realize a person in a coma could still hear, and they didn't know that hearing is the last sense to leave a person as they die. Jimmy's death on September 21, 1946, after an eight-year battle, left Mom widowed at age thirty-two with a young son to rear—but she wasn't single for long.

Months before his health declined and sent him to the hospital where he died, Jimmy went to see a communist speak. My father was also there. Every person who went was thrown into jail for the night. A while later, someone threw a party for everyone who'd been in jail together. Mom told me that woman after woman would come up to Jimmy, throw their arms around him, and kiss him. She was jealous, and with every kiss her anger grew. She decided that she would kiss the next man who walked through the door. It was my father. She must have made quite an impression, because he obviously kept track of her and was there when Jimmy died to help her with the funeral arrangements.

She married my dad, Bud, seven months later, on April 12, 1947, and Bud adopted Peter. Mom never spoke about their wedding and no pictures were taken of the happy couple. I was born exactly two years and four months later. Mom said I was wanted, but only on the condition I was a girl because she didn't want a boy who would "usurp Peter's position as your father's son."

Mom was so sick during her pregnancy with me that when the doctor admitted her to the hospital he said, "What did your husband inject you with? Poison?" Peter's IQ had dropped forty points, and his teacher was relieved when she saw my mother was pregnant and not dying. As a reward for his trauma, Mom allowed Peter to name me and he named me after a girl he had a crush on. Virginia was a terrible name for a child. I always hated my name. Virginia was hard to pronounce when I was little, and I was the butt of many bad jokes throughout my childhood and teens.

My parents had been married fourteen years when Dad died of a massive heart attack and Mom was a widow again at age forty-seven, this time left with two children to care for. His death turned Mom into a bitter, angry shadow of her former, happy self. Her grief froze inside her and left her with the emotional range of the two middle notes on an eighty-eight key piano. She never cried, not in front of me and not even when she was alone.

Maybe that's why when I was a child Mom said, "When you're an adult, your tear ducts dry up and you don't cry anymore." Perhaps she believed this was true. I tried to be like her and for a long time I shoved my tears down. In my twenties, after I started therapy, I was like a backed up garbage disposal, and every unshed tear began to fall.

Mom was strong for Goldie, Jimmy, and my dad while they were alive, but once they stopped breathing, she could not go near their dead bodies.

Perhaps another death, even the death of my dog, was too much for her. Maggie's death might have reminded Mom of her own vulnerability and how she had come close to death only three months before. Perhaps when she said, "You're lucky it wasn't me," she was crying out for her own mother. Mom loved her dad, but he was a benign, gentle man. They didn't share the close conversational relationship she experienced with her mother. The two of them would read books and discuss each one, and Mom missed not being able to do that with her mother for more than sixty years. Perhaps her words were an ineffectual attempt to warn me how much I was going to miss her after she was gone.

But when she said those words so soon after Maggie died and all these years after my dad died, I believed I would be better off with either of them instead of her.

———

My mother missed her own mother so much that she knew once she was gone, I'd miss her the rest of my life.

She'd never admit or discuss the issues that grow like nasty weeds between us. My role in our relationship has always been to be the one to bring up problems we need to discuss and work to minimize the large emotional distance that stood between us and shrouded our love.

Maggie's been gone three weeks now, and I can no longer tolerate our cold war.

"Mom, we're not getting along." Mom is at the kitchen sink, and I face her on the other side of the island. My chest flutters as I wait.

Mom peers over her shoulder at me before she turns around. "Tell me something I don't know," she says, her words dry as the desert dust.

"Okay, Mom, it's obvious." I tilt my head and give a curt nod. "But I don't know how to fix us."

She studies me as though she can read the words as they leave my lips.

I pause to gather courage. "Mom, I think we should see a therapist."

"Okay," she says with no hesitation.

She never ceases to surprise me. When I expect her to be

nice, she'll say something harsh. When I expect her to be harsh and withholding, she's willing and understanding. This relationship is a high-wire act requiring careful steps or we'll fall into an abyss because we have no net other than our intelligence and deep love.

I make an appointment with a psychologist who works with the geriatric population. I believe we need a knowledgeable professional who is aware of and comfortable with the emotional and physical issues my mother may be experiencing.

A week later Mom is sitting on the couch across the room of the therapist's office, but there is a lot more distance than floor space between us. Dr. Mark Bilkey's office is a warm rectangle with a large window at the back and one wall lined with bookshelves filled with psychology books. Dr. Bilkey, a handsome, tall man in his early forties with raven-black hair, sits in a leather chair, and I'm on the couch closest to him. After I've said hello and introduced my mother, Dr. Bilkey says, "Now tell me what brings you here."

"Maggie, my Golden Retriever died, and *she* doesn't seem to realize how much Maggie meant to me and how heartbroken I am." I glance over the top of my glasses at my mother.

"Of course I know what the dog meant to her," she says.

I turn to Dr. Bilkey, "If she understood how I felt about Maggie she would never call her 'the dog.'" My barely contained hostility drips like acid from each word.

Dr. Bilkey, being a good therapist, doesn't choose sides but forces us to work towards an understanding of each other.

"Ruth, can you understand that Maggie was more to Ginni than just a dog?"

Mom is quiet for a moment, then her brow furrows and her eyes soften. "Yes, now I can," she says to Mark.

"Ruth, you need to tell Ginni."

Mom turns to me and for the first time since Maggie died, I see concern in her expression. She rubs her clasped hands and clears her throat. "Ginni, honey, I'm so sorry. I do know how much Maggie meant to you. I recognized how hurt you were and I felt helpless. I had no idea what to do or say because you seemed so prickly. I was afraid I'd say the wrong thing, and then everything I did seemed wrong."

"Mom, I'm sorry too. I've been wrapped up in my own pain and haven't had the energy to explain to you what I wanted and needed from you." I close the abyss between us and sit next to her. "I love you, Mom." I put my arms around her and she grasps on to me. Mom is not a demonstrative person, especially in front of other people, and she doesn't hold on very long before she lets go.

Hindsight is always twenty-twenty. I might have prevented a lot of our problems had I realized that because I was hurt I wanted to crawl up inside myself and scream, but Mom's presence in my house made me think I had to hold back the screams. I resented her for forcing me to hide. Of course she didn't force me. I played my part in the dance we did, her wanting me to assure her that I loved her more than Maggie, and me wanting her to be the mother of my childhood who took away my hurts with a kiss, a hug, and some warm chocolate pudding.

We are both smiling by the end of the session, and we set up another appointment. I am filled with hope and believe we've been set back on the path of love and friendship we walked together before she moved in.

I had forgotten that there have always been potholes in our relationship.

Chapter 12:

Thanksgiving

*My two parents represent the single greatest influence on
my life. And if my dad had been there for me, it would
be the double greatest influence on my life.*
—Jarod Kintz, This Book Has No Title

*No matter how far we come, our parents are always
in us.*
—Brad Meltzer, The Inner Circle

THURSDAY, NOVEMBER 25, 1999

"Ginni, I need your nose."

I shake the glass spice jar and watch the green mist of poultry
seasoning float onto the stuffing mixture of cornbread, apples,
celery, pecans, and a splash of chicken broth. The bouquet of

parsley, sage, rosemary, and thyme takes me back to other holidays. Time stands still before I hop off the barstool to approach Mom, who's making apple pie. She lifts a spoonful of apples mixed with sugar, cinnamon, and lemon zest for me to sniff. I inhale the familiar, spicy fragrance. "I think it needs a little more cinnamon, Mom."

"I thought so, too, but wanted to check with you to make sure."

Before I return to my stuffing, the light breeze from the open window above the sink reminds me of what a treat fresh air is after long, hot summer days when the house is sealed like a tomb to keep out Hades-like temperatures. Today is a comfortable 72 degrees. Across the street, couples stroll with dogs of all sizes. A man rides by in a golf cart with his Labrador Retriever tethered by a leash. The dog's mouth is open and a pink tongue hangs off its whiskered muzzle. The petite lady with a long braid draped down her back isn't taking her usual walk with the black German shepherd whose back legs sway because of hip dysplasia. For some reason, I've always thought the dog isn't hers and belongs to people she works for. Their nonappearance bothers me because the dog seems old and in pain. I'm afraid their absence could mean he's gone, like my Maggie.

The sumptuous aroma of freshly baked pumpkin and apple pies fills the house, and my memory soon wafts back to my father. For a moment, a familiar ache squeezes my chest and I miss him. I wonder if Mom misses him or thinks about him, but I don't ask. We rarely talk about my father, and it's almost as if there's been an unwritten code to never bring up that other Thanksgiving when tragedy struck. Still, the event haunts me and continues to weave its fibers throughout the tapestry of my life.

Until that Monday, November 20, 1961, the Monday before Thanksgiving, each morning would be alive with the sounds and scents of my father and mother getting ready for the day.

Dad, in the master bathroom, would always shower and whistle the theme from the Academy Award–winning movie *Around the World in 80 Days*. It was a wistful, sweeping melody that spoke of the unstoppable, optimistic quest for the beloved. His jaunty whistle mixed with the sounds of water until he stepped out of the shower with a click of the door. Pretty soon came the *slap, slap* as he put Old Spice Aftershave on his face. In the kitchen, Mom would bustle about with pots and pans—bang, clang, and clatter. Bacon sizzled on the stove and fresh coffee rumbled in the percolator, and these sounds and smells were like a signal that called out, *Wake up, wake up.*

But that Monday before Thanksgiving when I was twelve years old, I didn't hear my father or my mother. I didn't smell Old Spice or bacon or coffee. There was no *Around the World in 80 Days*, no slap of aftershave, and no bang, clang, and clatter. Instead, the gray stillness of the house was all over and around me, its eerie shadows the only hint of morning. Rain pounded on the roof as if trying to get inside. Outside my window, the rain slashed on the concrete walkway.

I sat up in bed: Nancy Drew, girl detective, in search of a clue. My birch dresser, my desk, my bookcase—everything was in its place, but something was wrong. It was cold and rainy, and my orbit of predictability—the smells, the sounds, the routine—had slipped away.

I padded barefoot to my parents' room across the hall. Their door was closed and no light peeked from under the door. Other than the rain, there was nothing but silence.

I knocked on the door with a light touch.

"Mom? Dad?"

Nothing.

I took a deep breath and tried again.

"It's after 7:00," I called out, my voice a tentative squeak. Their voices were muffled, hers soft, his rough, hers calm, his on fire.

Mom opened the door just enough for me to see her face and a sliver of her body. She was sleepy, but beautiful as always in her pale green silk pajamas, not one of her reddish-blonde hairs out of place.

"Morning," she whispered, her voice husky and low from so many Chesterfield cigarettes.

"Morning, Mom. How come you're not up? It's kind of late. Is it okay if I come in?"

"Wait a sec until Dad has a chance to get his shorts on."

She checked over her shoulder a couple of times and eventually opened the door all the way.

I stepped slowly into the room, my head down but eyes up so I could keep an eye on Dad without being noticed.

I don't think Dad saw me. He was upset about something, moving in the quick long strides of a panther, his angry face dark and dangerous. He shoved the bottom of his white T-shirt, the one he usually wore when he went out on his boat, into his waistband and then yanked his belt through the loops of his khaki pants.

"Damn Peter for not sweeping the leaves off the roof when I asked him to," Dad erupted.

I never got used to Dad getting mad. I hated my father's anger because it scared me and I hated being scared. I didn't like feeling helpless or how my stomach hurt. His anger, so strong, so intense, made me hate him. And I hated hating someone I loved so much.

At first my father's anger was so consuming I didn't notice how rain dripped from the ceiling light near the foot of their bed, leaving most of their blanket soaked. I sat down on the one dry spot, away from the water and light, so I wouldn't be pulled into the eddy of my father's all too familiar anger.

"Bud, calm down." Mom glowered at Dad, her voice stern and words clipped. "You don't know if this has anything to do with Petey." She was always this way when it came to Peter. She protected him and stood up for him. She never saw anything wrong with him, never admitted he made any mistakes or even that he was cruel to my friends and me.

Peter, at eighteen years old, had started to challenge Dad's authority. They argued all the time, like two bulls, horns locked, struggling for power.

Dad plopped his big body down on Mom's pink chaise and tugged on his shoes. His face was hard. "Because of Peter," he bellowed, "I have to go outside in this rain and fix things." In a huff he pushed off the chaise and stomped from the room.

For a beat, Mom and I stood still, our eyes focused on the empty doorway as if Dad had sucked some of the air and life out of the room when he left. It was like that even when he went on business trips. Our lives revolved around him, and we would be a little lost until he returned.

Mom looked over at me and shrugged. I shrugged in the same way, a shared, non-verbal *Oh, well,* but even though I acted like her, it was her way, not mine. I tried to be like her, but ever since my body started to change, I hadn't been able to shrug off Dad's hot moods.

We'd seen Dad angry before. The only thing new was that this time the tsunami hit while we were all still half asleep. Mom inhaled, exhaled with a soft sigh, and became all business. "Ginni, go get ready for school." She was on her way to her closet even before I left the room.

What a lousy way to start the day I huffed as I trudged back to my room to get dressed. I had more important things to think about than Dad's anger. This was supposed to be a special day. I was going to play piano for my first period music class—my first performance ever. I'd never played for anyone except my piano teacher and family.

Mom's shrug didn't work. Even though I tried as hard as I could, it was never easy for me to pretend away bad things. I had become a good actress, or so I thought, but the confusing thoughts and uncomfortable feelings would settle into a heavy knot in my stomach and shoulders.

In my room, I put on my white blouse, gray jumper, white socks, and new black slip-on shoes. As I headed to the bathroom to brush my teeth and fix my hair, I halted mid-step when I heard Mom scream, "Bud! BUD!"

I ran to the pink master bathroom and found Mom with her forehead up against the glass of the window, looking into the backyard.

"BUD!' she shrieked even louder, and my ears rang with the sound of her shrill voice.

She pushed away from the window and flew past me.

I followed her out into the gloomy downpour.

We found Dad curled in a fetal position on the path to the patio. One more step and he would have made it to shelter. He'd ripped the thick gold necklace from his neck, and it lay on the ground next to him.

Mom bent down and called his name, her tone tentative and unfamiliar. I didn't understand what I was seeing or what this meant. I just knew it was bad. Back in 1961, death was hidden from children; it never seemed to happen to people unless they were ancient, and then everyone acted like the person had just disappeared.

Mom unfolded Dad's body and he rolled onto his back. "He's still breathing," she said.

I could see his chest moving up and down.

"Ginni, go wake up Peter," she instructed in a crisp voice, "and have him bring me a blanket."

I wasn't much of a runner, but I sprinted with newfound speed to the back door. As I reached for the handle, a voice stopped me.

"Birginia," said Ethel, our neighbor. "What's all the commotion?"

Ethel was in her bedroom, opposite our driveway. She always called me by the name I called myself when I was two years old and couldn't pronounce the "V."

"Oh, Ethel, something's happened to Dad," I said, my voice choked by a combination of being out of breath, fear, and tears. "Mom and I found him on the ground outside the patio and we can't wake him up."

"I'll call the Fire Department," she said. I didn't understand why she wanted to call the Fire Department when there was no fire, but I was in too much of a hurry to ask.

"I've got to get to Peter," I called to Ethel as I yanked the door open and dashed into the house. I ran through the kitchen and into the den, where I paused for a moment at Peter's doorway before walking into his stale, dark lair.

Peter was a lump in his bed.

I gave his shoulder a shake.

"Peter, Peter, wake up. Something's wrong with Dad." Peter rolled over and I stepped back.

"Huh?"

"Mom says you have to get a blanket and bring it outside," I yelled. "Dad's lying in the rain."

Peter sat up in his bed and rubbed his whole face with his hand.

"Come on." My voice was pinched and high. "Hurry—please!"

Peter didn't move. It's like my words were part of some dream he was having and he couldn't reach beyond the stupor of sleep. He was a zombie. Then it hit me: I didn't need him. I could help Mom myself.

I crossed the den to the linen closet in my parents' room and dug out a wool blanket. In a flash, like magic, I was back at my mother's side and handing it to her.

She cooed at Dad as she draped the blanket over his drenched body.

"Mom," I called into her fog, "I've got to tell Madelyn and her Dad not to wait for me."

It's so odd to remember the little things, how all the years of training to be polite and considerate came into play even when my world was spiraling out of orbit. Madelyn and I usually walked the forty-five minutes to school, but because we expected rain that day, we had planned for her dad, Mr. Davis, to drive us. And although I was in the middle of a crisis, I knew I couldn't let them wait for me.

I stood in the dining room and dialed Madelyn's number. As soon as I heard her voice, my words poured out in a rush and I twisted the cord around my finger, my wrist, my arm while I talked.

"Madelyn, it's me, Ginni. Something's happened to my dad and I won't be going to school."

"What's wrong?" The voice was not Madelyn's; it was her father's.

Did I even tell him what happened? I don't know. What I do know is that by the time I walked out the back door and reached my father, Mr. Davis was already there, at his side and pushing on my dad's chest.

A fire truck screeched up in front of the house and men rushed into the backyard.

Ethel showed up with her son, Barry, and they grabbed hold of me and pulled me to the front yard, away from my parents.

Peter was in the driveway, his hands cupped over his ears as he ran down the driveway and back up again, screaming at the top of his lungs. He sounded like an animal being tortured.

"Let me go," I hollered as I twisted against Ethel and Barry in a futile effort to loosen their grasp.

"You're better off staying here," Ethel cautioned, her grip tight on my arm.

"Please, I need—to—be—with—my—dad! I have to know what's being done to him. How he is."

I twisted and turned as I struggled against them, and ultimately got away.

Without looking back, I ran fast and hard through the puddles, up the driveway, and past Peter. Dad had been moved closer to the house, onto the small lawn just outside my bedroom windows, and three firemen were on the ground surrounding him. One was pushing on Dad's chest.

I stopped by my father's feet, and even though the experts later told us my father had died the moment he went down in our yard, I'll swear on my life that he opened his eyes and looked at me.

His once tanned, handsome face was a greenish-blue hue and the whites of his eyes were red and ragged, as though they'd been gnawed at. Sadness was in his eyes, too, a kind of despair and regret as if he were saying, *I'm sorry I'm leaving you.*

The night before was the last time we had spoken.

I had been watching Judy Garland in *A Star Is Born.* She sang "The Man That Got Away," which was all about nature becoming cold and bitter, stars no longer shining, and finding ourselves suddenly older because of losing a special man. Dad didn't want me to watch the rest of the movie and we argued. He wanted me to turn the TV off and go to bed. I insisted I see the end. He yelled. I resisted. It was the only argument I ever won. I got to stay up to watch Judy's husband, played by James Mason, kill himself by walking into the Pacific Ocean.

The next morning, death wasn't a movie. It was my own father who was going away. I didn't think of the future. I couldn't comprehend that the life I knew had drowned and that what was left to wash up on the shore had been transformed into something new and different. I didn't know there were no wishes, hopes, bargains, promises, or prayers that could turn that day into a simple nightmare from which I would awaken.

It was 1961, the beginning of a decade that started out with great promise and ended with our country in great turmoil: it began with a new, young President and beautiful First Lady, then went on to the Cuban Missile Crisis, the assassination of John F. Kennedy, the Watts Riots, the assassination of Martin Luther King, Jr., the unpopular Vietnam War, the assassination of Bobby Kennedy, and the first man walking on the moon.

Dad was alive for only Kennedy's inauguration.

I couldn't imagine all the birthdays, graduations, weddings, successes, and grandchildren my dad would never see. Or the times that I would, when sad, scared, or just needing to be held, crawl into a man's arms because the one man I wanted to hold me was no longer there. I didn't know that day was the first, but not last, time my heart would break. I didn't know that I would let go when I should hold on, hold on when I should let go, or that I would cry more for the end of relationships that should end than I would ever cry for the loss of my dad, and that one day I would realize the tears I'd shed over the years had all been for him. I was too young to know that only through living my life would I come to understand what I had both lost and gained that day.

I wanted it to be the day before, when Dad sat on his favorite green couch in the living room and listened to me play "Exodus" on the piano in preparation for my performance on Monday. The day Dad said how proud he was.

———

As my father looked at me from where he lay on the ground, while the firemen worked on him, my mother turned her gaze in my direction. There were no tears in her eyes, and I knew this meant we were to be strong; we don't cry, and we don't show people our feelings. But I could see what others never could. Mom looked lost and confused and almost like a child—younger than I was—and she was soaking wet in the rain that still kept coming down. She was just forty-seven, the mother of two children, and now widowed a second time.

In that moment, soaked to the bone by relentless rain, I couldn't know the mother I'd known my whole life was also dying that morning. Her ever-present smile, gone. Her laughter, gone. Her playfulness, gone. The life she knew—her life as a wife, part of a popular, handsome couple that dressed up in their best clothes and went out to parties—gone.

My once happy mother would soon become bitter. She would feel abandoned by her friends and convince herself it was because she was no longer part of a couple. I always thought they stopped calling because she was angry and unpleasant, but I never said anything to her because I was afraid she'd get mad at me.

I was too young to consider what it meant to be forty-seven years old and watch your second husband die. I didn't know all the hurt I would feel when she focused her attention and love on

Peter, how awful it would feel to be the forgotten child, and how this would make me long even more for my father's love.

I didn't understand the way our roles would change, or all the fights we'd have, and how our love for each other would still somehow remain stronger than any other storms we'd weather.

I never paid much attention to the ordinary days of my life because I didn't understand they could be taken away, or how miraculous and valuable they were.

I thought they'd always be there.

———

The space between 1961 and 1999 seems brief and our lives have blurred by at a faster-than-the-speed-of-light pace.

These two Thanksgivings are similar to me because death has visited, and I am anything but grateful on this day we are supposed to celebrate gratitude. Life without Maggie is a sad emptiness, and I struggle with how unfair it feels that she suddenly disappeared from my life. Dad and Maggie held special places in my heart that have been left forever hollow without them.

In 1961, Thanksgiving was the day after we buried my dad. We barely touched the two tasteless turkeys prepared for us by well-meaning friends. Those turkeys mocked our anguish with memories of the last happy Thanksgiving celebration we'd had, when our family and all of its members were alive. Today, Maggie's absence is all around me as we prepare the meal.

After Mom takes her pumpkin and apple pies out of the oven, I put in the stuffed turkey. Our lives go on as though there never was that other Thanksgiving, or that Mom almost died this year. We go on as though we will always go on.

And tonight and forever, Thanksgiving means my mother and apple pies.

Chapter 13:

One Millennium Is As Good As The Next

Time is not measured by the passing of years but by what one does, what one feels, and what one achieves.

—Jawaharlal Nehru

1999–2003

It's New Year's Eve and 1999 passes into 2000 while we sleep. When I open my eyes in the morning, a new millennium lies ahead and the century I was born into is gone. Mom didn't die in 1999, and despite dire Chicken Little warnings of a Millennium Bug, computers around the world function as before, making me glad I hadn't spent any extra money on what some called a necessary fix. My computer continues to hum along better than my life.

Mom and I settle into a routine that extends from 1999 and into the next few years.

The first year, Mom attends a watercolor painting class once a week at the La Quinta Senior Center. It was my idea that she take the class, and when I see what she is able to create after not having painted for more than sixty years, my awe for her talent mixes with sadness for the other things she either never allowed herself or that life didn't afford her the opportunity to achieve. She selects the most beautiful color combinations, bold and filled with a vibrant energy I never see in her.

"That's beautiful, Mom," I tell her, and I can see that my words are a tonic that makes her look proud. I'm glad I encouraged her to go because she'd always said that she was a good artist when she was young.

"Oh, it's okay," she says, but I know she feels proud of herself.

I wish I could say our roles had reversed from when I was a child and brought home pictures to share and Mom would shower me with praise, but I inherited none of her artistic talent and don't recall ever bringing a picture home. I always visualized one thing in my head but wasn't able to convert my internal image into anything recognizable.

I now put my lack of artistic talent to good use with the grieving children at my Center when we do an art-based activity. If a child says they don't want to draw because they aren't any good, I say, "You know I can't draw and I'm going to do it." The girl or boy always smiles with an energetic nod, then picks up a crayon and begins to create a picture. And just like my mother, the children discover the artist within.

On Mondays, Mom plays Pan, which is short for Panguingue, a rummy game played with eight decks of cards minus all eights, nines, and tens. Tuesdays and Fridays, she plays bridge. If she could find more games, she would play bridge five days a week.

"You should try it, Ginni," she says one evening while we are eating dinner.

I shake my head in protest. "I remember when I was a kid, you and Dad and your friends would play poker and the house overflowed with happy voices and laughter. I was nine or ten years old when you took up bridge, and instead of laughing, everyone yelled at each other. That's when I decided I had no interest in a game that made people angry."

"Well, it's a wonderful game and *I* think it's a lot of fun." She purses her lips and turns her attention back to her dinner and her book.

Every Thursday, Mom gets her nails and hair done. She comes home each week with her hair perfectly coiffed, unlike the stick-a-bowl-over-her-head hairstyles her Los Angeles hairdresser always did. She looks younger and healthier than she has in years. No one would ever guess she's eighty-five and almost died six months ago.

I continue to work eighteen-hour days seven days a week, with a rare break to go out with friends. I take Mom to dinner at least once a week, usually to Sammy's, which is our favorite. Conversations are always better over a Messy Sundae.

Mom's independence allows me to feel free, and for the most part we get along well with the occasional outbursts of mother-daughter conflict that I've come to learn are far from atypical of this complex parent-child relationship. Every time this happens, I feel like the worst person/daughter in the world. I am often impatient and forget she is old and her time on this earth limited. If I remembered, wouldn't I be nicer and less reactive?

I wish it were that simple or easy.

I don't want to argue. I don't want to not like my mother and I don't want to feel this conflict. Even if I think she started the argument, I always end up feeling guilty. I feel like I'm bad because I'm the daughter and my job is to protect and be good to my mother. Yet I can't protect her from me.

Sometimes as I skulk away from our latest rumble and my internal voice tells me I should be nicer, I should be more patient, I should be kinder, I think of the words of Ram Dass: *No one likes to be should upon.* I also recall the day my friend Sue first met Mom.

———

Sue, a pretty, strawberry blonde licensed clinical psychologist, lost her own mother three years ago, when Sue was thirty-three. As soon as I introduced them, Sue and Mom fell into the easy conversation of two old friends who hadn't seen each other in a long while. Sue was all smiles, touching my mother's arm and laughing as though Mom had said the funniest thing she'd ever heard. I watched from a distance like a petulant child left out of the conversation her best friends were having.

When Sue and I were outside the house walking towards her black car, she said, "You should be nicer to your mother."

"Yes, I know." I nodded in agreement as guilt and shame spread all over me like a bad rash.

"She won't always be here," Sue said as she stood by her car.

I could hardly see Sue because of the tears that filled my eyes.

"I know," I heard my voice crack. "But what would you do if she were your mother?"

"Oh, I'd kill myself," Sue said without a moment's hesitation, her words a rapid-fire validation.

I laughed, relieved because she wasn't blind to my mother's personality, and she could see I wasn't the sole cause of all of our problems.

Even so, her words stay with me because she was right. My mother won't always be here and I need to close the emotional space between us.

———

Many things occur during the years 2000–2003, but only a few change our lives:

On December 23, 2000, I bring home Sunshine, a beautiful, six-week-old Golden Retriever with the face of an angel. I fall in love right away with the puppy I nickname Sunny, but Mom is dubious. She does her best to withhold her affection until the puppy kisses and tail wags do their job and her heart opens.

In June of 2002, I adopt my friend's Golden Retriever Sophie, who is six months older than Sunny. Sophie immediately establishes her dominance through aggressive attacks and Sunny soon learns to stand up for herself. They snarl and snap and wrestle as though dueling to the end, only to stop and lie down next to each other like dear sisters or best friends. They remind me of the honesty of children before they are taught to pretend, and I imagine this conversation:

"I hate you."

"I hate you, too."

"Okay, let's go play."

Mom and I are somewhat like Sunny and Sophie, without the overt snarls, bites, and *I hate yous.*

———

In the spring of 2003, my heart is ready to give love another chance. The desert is not fertile ground for a woman in her fifties unless she's interested in a man in his seventies or eighties. With old age up close and personal in my home, I know that's not what I want. My ex-mother-in-law says older men are "only interested in a nurse or a purse." Because a pretty and successful close friend of mine met a wonderful man online, I decide to give it a try.

In July, I sign up. Once my picture is posted, men begin to contact me. I'm old-fashioned, even in this new age, and can't bring myself to be the one to contact a man first. I am grateful for my degree in psychology because I can recognize and weed out the narcissists, abusers, and potential stalkers. I like being able to meet men without having to brush my teeth, get out of my pajamas, put on makeup, or even comb my hair, but after three weeks of online dating with men who are egotistical or want to start fights before we've even met, I'm about ready to close my account.

On the morning of July 30, a message arrives that will change my life.

"Don't delete me. I'm planning to move to the desert."

He lives in the Dallas–Fort Worth area of Texas, which is much farther than the geographical range I indicated on my profile. His name is Bob. I don't think much of his picture. *He looks like a stuffy accountant.* But I do like what he says about himself and what he wants out of life. He's a widower and clearly loved his wife. "I've known love and want to experience it again."

I write back and we soon learn we grew up only a few miles from each other, me in West Los Angeles and Bob in Culver City. After four days of online communication, Bob writes, "I'd like to put a voice to your face. May I call you?"

I think this is cute and only much later find out he was tired of typing two fingers at a time. He calls that evening and we talk for more than an hour, not like people who've never met but like friends and lovers who've always known each other. And although I'm not willing to fall in love with a man I've only met online and talked to on the phone, I can't help feeling he's the one.

A week later, we rendezvous in the lobby of the Miramonte

Hotel, a resort close to my house. Meeting him in person is like connecting with someone I've always known, and we fall into easy conversation. We spend the whole day together, and that evening we go out to dinner with a group of his friends. Bob had arranged this before we met, and afterwards I jokingly ask him if they held up score cards to take a vote on me. We see each other the next night and then two days later to celebrate my birthday. He leaves for Texas the following day and we talk on the phone every day, sharing what we've been doing. We never speak of feelings other than to say we look forward to seeing each other again.

When he returns to the desert ten days later, I pick him up at the Palm Springs Airport and bring him home to meet my mother. His easygoing personality, mixed with a bit of southern charm, wins her over. Mom is interesting and playful with him, showing signs of the mom I knew before Dad died. She flirts, asks questions, laughs at things Bob says, and smiles in a way I haven't seen in a long time. Later she tells me she approves of Bob, and of course I am pleased.

When Mom behaves well with people, I relax. I like her and am proud to be the daughter of this intelligent and interesting woman.

Mom's health has been good since 2000, so I'm not concerned about her being alone with the dogs when Bob invites me to join him in Boston where he will participate in a charity golf tournament. We are getting serious about our relationship, and I want to spend time alone with him.

First stop: his home in Texas and a party with his friends. Despite believing that my work and an understanding of grief give me a leg up when it comes to dealing with a widower and his friends, I'm a little nervous about meeting all these people who were close to Bob's deceased wife, Flo. I'm concerned they will compare me to her and make the types of insensitive comments

I've heard about from other girlfriends and wives of widowers. None of this happens. Bob's friends are nothing but gracious, and their kindness puts me at immediate ease.

Now that I'm in his home, it's clear that Bob is still in love with Flo. Her photographs are all over the house, her smile and the closeness of the two of them in the pictures look out at me as if to say, "He's mine and always will be. Look how happy and in love we are." The embroidered *Happiness is being married to your best friend* pillow on a bench in his bedroom snipes at my self-confidence about this new relationship.

Bob acts different towards me once we get to Boston. He's pleasant and always a gentleman, and although we share a bed and make love, by the time I get on the plane in Texas to head back to the desert without him, I feel as though he's slipped away. Timing is everything, and in our case perhaps it was not a good idea to make our first trip together within days of the third anniversary of his wife's death.

Mom's already asleep by the time I get home. I'm anxious to talk to her but have to wait until the next morning. She was a widow when she married Dad, and I want to know what it was like for her to love someone new. I trust in her wisdom, which has helped me find my way many times when I've been lost or scared.

The next morning, while we sip coffee, we have the chance to catch up.

"How was your trip?" she asks with a smile and lilt in her voice. Still wearing her polyester satin, bright-colored nightshirt, which is short enough to show off her long, tapered calves and slender ankles, she perches on a bar stool with her legs crossed.

"It was a lot of fun. But I'm sure Bob is still in love with his deceased wife and I don't know what to do." I sit on the bar stool next to her, already dressed for work.

"I'm glad you had a good time."

"What was it like for you with Dad?" I ask, because I want to know if her love for Jimmy came between them in any way.

"With Dad?"

"Yes, you were a widow when you met Dad. What was it like to be with someone new?"

"I started seeing your father soon after Jimmy died, and although I loved Jimmy, he never came between me and your father."

"Never?" That seems impossible to me.

"Jimmy had been sick a very long time and I'd done all my grieving by the time he was gone. He was dead and your father was alive," she says in her usual straightforward, blunt manner. She takes a sip of her coffee and puts the mug down on the counter. Her blue eyes are dark, and although she looks at me, for a moment she seems to be far away. She shakes her head and refocuses her attention on me.

"Did you compare Dad to Jimmy?"

"Absolutely not. They were two different men, and when I started my life with your father, I never looked back. I loved your father completely."

She walks over to the coffee pot, pours another cup, and turns back towards me. "Give Bob some time. He cares about you and he's a good man. Be patient. He knows he's lucky he's met a girl like you."

"Thanks, Mom." I hop off the stool, wrap my arms around her, and kiss her cheek, grateful I could share this with her. Grateful to be with a mother I love and trust.

Chapter 14:

A Slice of Life

*Dogs are wise. They crawl away into a quiet corner and
lick their wounds and do not rejoin the world until they
are whole once more.*

—Agatha Christie

JANUARY 2004

Days continue to speed by and blur one into the next. This late
January morning, warm and bright, gives no inkling that my life
is about to be hijacked. No hint that today's event portends the
big changes destined to enter our lives this year like an unwelcome gang of escaped felons.

I am alone at the office at a pink metal desk, one of two I purchased at a used office furniture store when I started the Center. The

desk rests against a wall under a window with open blinds. As I gaze at the sealed shutters hiding the interior of the law office across the walkway, I struggle to find the words to complete an article about Carolyn, a high school student who lost her mother when she was five and was orphaned at age seventeen when her father died just before her senior year. Her school counselor, recognizing she needed help with her grief, called me, and I have been meeting with her for more than a year. Carolyn decided to help other children, went through our training, and is now one of my best facilitators.

I lean back in my comfortable chair and stare out the window as if the pinkish-beige, two-story structure across the small path will offer inspiration.

The jingle of the phone jolts me from my thoughts. Although I work with grieving people and am always ready for whatever sad story may wait for me at the other end of the phone line, I am not prepared for this call.

"Thank you for calling The Mourning Star Center, Dr. Simpson speaking."

"Dr. Simpson, this is Onkar, your dry cleaner." Onkar is from India and speaks with an accent.

"Onkar?"

"Yes, yes. It's your mother." His voice is higher than normal and his words much faster and sharper.

"What? What's wrong?" My heart is on a race.

"She had an accident."

"Accident?" I'm surprised my voice remains placid. Mom would say I'm using my *professional voice.*

"Yes, yes. She's okay, but you must come right away."

Everything slows down and simultaneously speeds up. I grab my keys and purse and without knowing how I get there, I park my car in front of the cleaners. I dash out of the car and as soon as

I step through the front door, the heat and chemical smell assault me. The only sound is the whoosh of steam from the electric iron.

Onkar, a dark-skinned man with black hair and a thick moustache, stands behind the counter. When he sees me, he emits loud sounds and rapid hand gestures before he calms down. Once he does, I can understand what he is saying.

"She hasn't complained. She just sits there, quiet." Onkar nods towards my mother, who is perched on a chair at the front window, pressing a cloth to her shin. Except for the bloodied crimson towel, Mom looks perfect, not one hair out of place. Her expression is peaceful.

I squat down so my face is level with hers. "What happened, Mom?" I touch her shoulder with concern.

"The car door hit my leg while I was putting my clothes in," she says with as much emotion as she might evince reading a grocery list. Her face remains serene and smooth, not a grimace in sight or a hint of discomfort or pain.

"I'm so sorry, Mom," I say, dry tears behind my words.

"This is so stupid." She tsks and sighs. She doesn't say she's disgusted with herself, but I know from the past that she is.

The cloth on her leg is bloody, but not a drop has reached her white socks or Keds.

I force myself to remain composed in spite of feeling shaky inside.

"Let me take a peek," I say, even though I don't want to look at her bloody leg. I do what needs to be done. We are at our best in a crisis: I'm attentive and patient, and she's sweet and compliant, like the good little girl she was before life slung its arrows at her heart.

As she unwraps the cloth, I try not to gasp at the long gash. I will myself not to wince, but I'm filled with anxiety about the wound.

"Mom, we need to get you to the emergency room *right now*." I moderate my tones to match her blasé attitude.

"Okay," she nods.

I ask Onkar to help me get her to my car.

With gentle care, we help her out of the chair and walk her to the car. Until Mom had the blood clot and then began to live with me, I was arrogant in my belief that I was more enlightened because years of therapy taught me to speak ad nauseam about my every emotion or thought. But therapy taught me nothing about living. As I observe the dignity with which my mother handles scary or painful situations, I wonder if her way of just accepting the next thing and getting on with life is better than my verbal upchucking of emotions.

Eisenhower Medical Center, named after our thirty-fourth President, who was a desert resident, should be less than a ten-minute drive, but the roads are clogged with tourist traffic.

"Damn snowbirds," I say as I pound the steering wheel. I take in a cleansing breath to focus and relax. Snowbirds are mostly wealthy people who come to their second home in the desert to escape the cold. Today they're just an annoying impediment to my ability to get my bloody mom to a doctor. When yet another car cuts me off and slams on the brakes, "Asshole" slips out before I can stop it.

I glance over at Mom, who doesn't react. I hope that means she didn't hear me. *At least I didn't say "Fucking asshole."*

Twenty-five minutes later, we reach the Emergency Department. There are no other cars parked, which I hope means we won't have a long wait. "Mom, wait in the car while I find someone to get us a wheelchair to take you in."

"I can walk," she says, and tries to get up.

"I know you can, but this will be easier for both of us. Okay?"

"Oh, all right," she huffs.

I'm in and out of the building in minutes. "The woman at the reception desk told me to go to the Wound Care Department, which is in another building."

When I park again, Mom wants to walk on her own. We check in, and after a brief wait are escorted by a hefty, young, dark-haired man into a rectangular room large enough to hold a classroom of students. Two silver medical tables are in front of a window.

"Sit here, Mrs. Simpson." He gestures to the table closest to the door. "The doctor will be in to see you in a moment," he says as he leaves the room.

As I help Mom onto the table, she purses her lips.

"Are you okay, Mom?"

"Of course. This is nothing." She straightens up. "Remember, *I* get my teeth drilled with no Novocain."

"That's because Uncle Henry wouldn't use it. When I'd ask him to give me the Novocain he'd always say the discomfort of Novocain when it wears off is worse than the short pain of drilling."

"Well, I trained myself not to *feel* the pain. I have a strong will."

"I know you do. Stronger than me, Mom, that's for sure . . . Uncle Henry was wrong."

She smiles. Mission accomplished, I got her mind away from her leg. I preen, but only a wee bit, as I bask in her smile.

The door squeaks open and a pretty blonde woman in a white doctor's coat enters, followed by a tall woman in lavender scrubs.

"I'm Dr. Miller and this is my assistant, Barbara," she says. "Hello, Mrs. Simpson. How are you today?"

"I've been better, Doctor." Mom casts her eyes toward her leg.

Dr. Miller unwraps the cloth from her leg and says something to Barbara, who retrieves a silver tray filled with bottles, tubes, scissors, gauze, bandages, and other items.

"Pay attention," Dr. Miller says as she looks over at me, "because you're going to have to be responsible for your mother's care between visits with us."

I lean in to get a better view. Dr. Miller turns her attention back to my mother but continues to speak to me.

"First you wash the wound with a saline solution. If you have contact lens solution, use that, because it's pure saline." She pours a good amount of it on Mom's shin. The cut is three or four inches of raw skin. My stomach rolls as I watch, but I try to keep a neutral expression.

"We want the wound to stay moist. We don't want a scab to form, so we'll put this cream on the wound and cover it with a gauze dressing pad, then wrap it with self-adherent wrap the way I'm doing." She pulls the wrap over and around Mom's leg a few times, then asks, "Do you understand?"

I tell her I do, paying close attention to what she is doing.

"Her dressing must be changed every day until we see you again. Before you leave, stop at the front desk and make appointments to come back no later than three days from now and then once a week for the next four weeks."

I'm fascinated that we shouldn't let a scab form, and assure her I will take good care of Mom as I help her up and head toward the car.

⌒

Over the weeks I care for Mom's leg, a light brown scab appears but never hardens, and eventually morphs into a healed area with the mere hint of a scar, much less noticeable than I expected from a cut so severe.

I wonder if this could be the same for people. What if we didn't allow the hard scabs to form over our emotional wounds? Would we remain soft and able to forgive and let go, rather than carry the burden of unresolved anger? The more I consider this, I realize that scabs form a fortress against all perceived assaults yet help continue the separation.

Maybe I've become a hard scab with Mom, quick to rush to anger to protect myself in many of our encounters during the last few years. Perhaps if I softened, I would be more open and able to heal without leftover hard edges. Maybe this would allow me to listen to my mother with kindness and patience.

I wish there were a saline solution available to soften the scabs on my heart.

———

When the Titanic hit the iceberg, passengers had no idea the jolt they felt signaled the beginning of the end of many of their lives. And although my mother's cut leg seemed a minor thing, it signaled the onset of more health issues and our entrance into what I came to call "Death's Waiting Room."

PART 3:

IN DEATH'S WAITING ROOM

. . . .

Life is a succession of lessons which must be lived to be understood.

—Helen Keller

Chapter 15:

True Grit

*How much grit do you think you've got? Can you quit
a thing that you like a lot?*

—Edgar Albert Guest

SATURDAY, FEBRUARY 28, 2004

Days fold one into the next and our routines lull me into a false
sense of security about our future.

Don't go back to sleep, Rumi's poem warns, and yet I do.

I'm halfway across the house, headed towards the garage and
lunch with a friend. The buttery scent of eggs and toast cooked
earlier this morning greets me as I near the kitchen.

"Ginni!"

Mom's voice startles me, and I suck in air and hold my
breath, a bad habit. I pause mid-step in front of the kitchen, and
as I pivot to my right a silent snort escapes as I release my breath.

"Mom? What are you doing home? I thought you'd already left for bridge."

Mom leans back against the white tile next to the sink where the two counters meet at an angle. She holds up her keys with her right hand. "Take my car keys. I can't drive anymore." She's somber, mouth turned down, blue eyes dim, voice strong.

"What?" I hear her words but they don't compute. Mom loves to drive.

"I can't do it anymore."

"What do you mean 'you can't do it anymore'?"

"I got confused and couldn't remember how to get where I was going so I turned around and came home." Her voice cracks and she covers it with a cough. She folds down into herself and for a moment stares at the floor. Then, as though a puppeteer has pulled a string of interior strength, her chest expands and she unfolds and stands as straight and strong as a majestic redwood tree.

"I'm so sorry, Mom," I say in a gentle whisper.

Mom has made a huge decision. I am fortunate she is a realist. She always has been, and that trait does not fail us now. Most parents hold on to those car keys long after they should stop driving and force their children to wrest them from them like thieves preying on innocents.

Just last summer, in mid-July, an eighty-six-year-old man drove his car into a crowd of people at the Santa Monica Third Street Promenade farmer's market. In less than ten seconds he had killed ten people and injured another sixty-three. He said he accidentally put his foot on the accelerator instead of the brake and couldn't stop the car when he tried to brake. Ever since that incident and all the chatter on TV and in the newspapers about the diminished capacity of elderly drivers, I had been concerned about Mom. I dreaded the day when I would be forced to take her car keys and tell her she could no longer drive. I expected a war, nuclear.

Because of her pragmatic courage and dignity, we never had to fight this battle. She reminds me of my favorite Rilke poem, "The Man Watching." Like Rilke's man in the poem, my mom bends to the large things in life and no longer fights with the small. Those small things diminish us, while a challenge as large as Mom's decision to never drive again helps us grow. I admire my mother for her choice to let go of something she loves and to accept this painful new reality with neither a complaint or a hint of self-pity. I'm in awe of how she has grown from each challenge life has thrown at her this past year.

⌣‒‒‒

Some of my earliest memories are of my mother driving her car, one manicured hand on the wheel, a Chesterfield cigarette nestled between her second and third fingers, and a smile on her painted red lips. Her fingers, long and tapered, were strong enough to hold up a family and gentle enough to rub my head and soothe me when I was a sick child. I wanted long nails painted bright red just like my mom's.

⌣‒‒‒

My steps are slow as I walk across the kitchen and stop in front of Mom with my right hand extended palm up. She drops the keys in and I fist my hand around them.

I lean into her, wrap my arms around her, and kiss her warm cheek. "I'm so sorry, Mom. I'm proud of you for making this decision." Proud isn't a big enough word to describe my admiration and relief. She's done me a big favor and I know it. Thanks to her I will never be required to face an ugly day I was certain lay ahead of us.

She doesn't say anything. She can't. This is too big and she's already said a lot for her.

"Do you want me to take you to your card game?"

She shakes her head.

"How about I buy you lunch? We can go to Sammy's for a Messy Sundae."

"No. I think I'll just go to my room and read." She picks her black purse up off the counter, and I watch as she crosses the kitchen, turns left, and disappears down the hallway to her room.

I didn't see today coming, and I can't move from where I stand. My head shimmers back and forth, and I absentmindedly pet Sunny and Sophie, who seem to have appeared from out of nowhere. I travel back in time, remembering all the places Mom drove me when I was a child—the movies, shopping, doctor and orthodontist appointments, and dance lessons cut short due to my lack of talent. I was a child, so of course I didn't realize having a chauffeur was a privilege that would end the day I got my driver's license. Seventy-five years Mom's driven without a ticket, and today she said good-bye with few words and little emotion. I admire her dignity and grace—her grit.

I don't realize that a huge tectonic shift has occurred.

I will soon.

And this time I won't be able to go back to sleep.

Chapter 16:

Nowhere and Everywhere

Do the shells still hear the sea, though they are in pieces?
—L.L. Barkat

MARCH 2004

Since the day Mom handed over her car keys, I pay attention to everything about her: What she says, the tone of her voice, her facial expressions, and how she moves. I observe little change, and because her routines remain the same—card games twice a week, hair and nail appointments on Thursday—I convince myself she's fine.

The illusion doesn't last long.

On the morning of the 15ᵗʰ, the Ides of March, the day Caesar was told to beware, the veil is removed from my eyes. The moment I enter the kitchen, I know.

Mom stands in front of the coffee maker frozen and posed like a mannequin, her face devoid of all expression. Blank in a way I have never seen. She's not here, there, or anywhere.

"Mom?"

She doesn't react to the click of Sophie's toenails across the tile floor. Her face is absent—vacant—as though everything she's always been has fled to a faraway, invisible land. Sophie stops at her side and nuzzles Mom's hand with her wet nose. This seems to rouse Mom, and her blue eyes flicker to life.

She turns towards me, her movement incremental. She stares with a puzzled expression and says nothing.

"Mom? Are you okay?"

She starts to speak but what she says makes little sense and her voice trails off mid-sentence, like she's a robot and someone pulled the plug.

I rush over, touch her arm, and lean into her. "Mom?"

She looks at me and her eyes register no recognition. Before I can say anything, she's back and her azure eyes are alive and alert.

"Good morning, Ginni. I didn't see you come in."

I smile with relief. Mom's with me again, and for these special moments, I am less alone.

I want—no, need—to believe she's okay, and I tell myself this was nothing. I pour another a cup of coffee and return to my bedroom to get ready for work.

Twenty minutes later I'm back to refill my coffee. Mom stands where I left her, the switch off again. When I speak to her, she seems confused. She doesn't know how she got in the kitchen or why she's there.

I escort her to her bedroom and settle her on her bed.

I suspect she has some form of dementia. I have to get her to a doctor as soon as possible. Some dementias are reversible if caught soon enough, and since this is the first day this has happened—if I discount two weeks ago, when Mom was too lost to drive—whatever she's got must be in its early stage.

Although I don't believe this is an emergency, I do feel a sense of urgency.

I call Mom's internist and explain our situation. She refers me to Dr. Jacob Dillon, a neurologist in Indian Wells who she claims is the best in the desert.

Two days later, we are in the doctor's waiting room, a room as small, tight, and drab as I feel. Mom and I sit together on a yellow loveseat. Mom's legs are crossed at the ankle and her hands are folded in her lap like a good girl. She ignores the paperback book she brought. I have a clipboard cradled in my hands, and fill out a form with Mom's information. When I've finished, I walk over to the receptionist and place the clipboard on the counter.

"Thank you." She smiles and pulls the clipboard down towards her desk. "Dr. Dillon will be with you in just a few more minutes."

Before I return to my seat, I select one of the pamphlets on the wall that's supposed to tell me all I need to know about Alzheimer's.

Time seems to have stopped as we continue to wait. Mom never opens her book and I read the same few words of the pamphlet over and over again with not one iota of information reaching my awareness or memory. Maybe I'm the one who should see the doctor.

"Mrs. Simpson," a woman's voice calls out.

"Yes, that's us. Come on, Mom," I say in my sweet-daughter

voice, and I help her off the couch. We join the slender, dark-haired woman clad in periwinkle blue scrubs and black clogs.

"I'm Martha, the doctor's assistant. Please come with me."

We trail her through a narrow hallway stacked to the ceiling with gray lateral file cabinets on the right filled with a mess of manila files stuffed with paper.

She opens a door at the end of the hall on the left and with a sweep of her right arm indicates we should enter before her. The shallow gray room has a drab, popcorn-paneled ceiling that gives the room the appeal of a prison cell. Too little light seeps in from the small window to provide any relief from the oppression.

"Mrs. Simpson, hop up on the table," Martha says to Mom, then looks at me and adds, "You can sit in the chair next to the table. I'll let the doctor know you're ready for him."

"Thank you," Mom and I say in unison.

A few minutes later, Dr. Dillon, a tall, tan, handsome man with sandy brown hair streaked with gray, enters and strides over to Mom with his hand extended. "Mrs. Simpson, I'm Dr. Dillon." His silky voice is soft as freshly laundered sheets.

Mom holds out her hand in a genteel Scarlett O'Hara gesture. Her posture straightens and her chest puffs out. She reminds me of a seductress as she looks up at the doctor, her eyes filled with desire.

"Hello, Dr. Dillon," she purrs back at him like a cat who wants her tummy scratched. She sidles her body closer into his.

Did she just bat her eyelashes? Who is this woman? I'm amused to see this side of her. If she was this way with my dad, I don't remember, because he's been dead forty-three years.

Dr. Dillon glances at me and says, "You must be her daughter."

"Yes. My name is Virginia," I say, my voice reserved, the demeanor I use when acting in my professional capacity. I watch his every move so I can assure myself my mother is in good hands.

After he's listened to her heart and lungs, looked into her eyes and ears, and checked her blood pressure, he takes a clipboard off the counter behind him and says, "Well, Mrs. Simpson, I'd like to ask you a few questions, if that's okay with you."

"Sure." The word glides from Mom's pouty lips.

He looks down at the clipboard then up, clears his throat, and asks, "What's today's date?"

"Don't you know?" Mom answers.

I tilt my head down and cover my nose and mouth to stifle my smile.

"Yes, of course I do. But I want to know if you know."

She clears her throat and rubs her hands as though she's washing them. "It's—it's—March."

"Yes, it is March. Do you know the day and year?"

"The year?" She looks up and sighs. "It's 2000."

"Okay. Now, do you know what day is today?"

"Today. Today's Monday."

I know it's a cliché to say it, but my heart sinks, and as it does, uncomfortable, sad chemicals scamper up my throat. It's Wednesday, not Monday, and the year is 2004. The doctor is assessing her, and I have to remain a neutral observer. I can't help her out, much as I want to. It's what I do. I fix things for people, but I can't fix my own mother.

"Now, Mrs. Simpson—"

"Call me Ruth," she interrupts in a sultry voice.

"Ruth. Can you tell me what city we're in?"

"Los Angeles. No, that's not right. That's where I used to live. We're in the city where my daughter lives." She turns towards me for help. I want to offer a lifeline with *Indian Wells* written in bold letters, but I am forced to let her flounder. The doctor doesn't push her on this, just marks something on the sheet of paper.

"Now, Ruth, I'm going to say three words."

"Only three."

She hasn't lost her dry sense of humor.

He smiles. "Yes, Ruth, only three. Pay attention. Ball, flag, tree." He pauses between each word. "Can you repeat the words I've just said?"

"Ball . . ."

Silence. She sits still except for an increase in the hand washing.

"Ball," the doctor prompts.

"Yes, ball."

"And what else?"

"Ball and—oh, this is silly!" She shakes her head and dismisses him with a wave of her hand.

"Okay," the doctor says, his voice neutral and even. He checks the clipboard then says, "I'd like you to count backwards by seven, beginning with one hundred."

"I've never been good with numbers, but I'll try. One hundred, ninety-three . . ." She stops. She fidgets in her seat and looks down at her wrung-out hands.

Eight-six, Mom. Eight-six. I try to will her to read my mind and hear the answer.

Dr. Dillon must sense her discomfort, because he stops the questions and speaks to her in calm, measured tones. "That's okay. You did fine." I'm grateful that he's given her a life rope and way out of the humiliation I assume she feels. Mom has always prided herself on her intellect.

He turns to me and as though Mom is no longer in the room says, "I think your mother has had TIAs, small strokes, which have caused some early stage dementia. I'm going to prescribe Aricept, which should help with her memory. There's something important you need understand about Aricept. Once she starts to take it, she can never stop, because if she does, she can never take it again. Are we clear on this?"

"Yes, Doctor."

"Good." He writes out the prescription and hands the small paper to me. "I'd like to see your mother in two weeks."

Later I will wonder why I didn't insist that he order a CAT scan or MRI. I should have known these tests were necessary, because I've taken courses on aging, dementia, and end of life. Maybe the reason I wasn't more persistent is because I was trained as a child to never question authority and trusted the medical community to know what to do.

"Thank you, Dr. Dillon." I help Mom off the table. She doesn't say a word as we walk down the hall, stop to make another appointment, or drive back to the house. Once we're home, she goes to her room and turns on the TV. The dogs join her and I leave for the pharmacy to fill her prescription, feeling weighed down by sadness and fear about what lies ahead of us.

During the next few days, I don't notice any significant change. Sometimes Mom is lucid, her old self, and other times she's as vacant as an empty house.

About a week after we've seen the doctor, we're in the kitchen, the place where we always seem to meet. Mom says, "We've been together many times. Sometimes you've been the mother but last time we weren't mother and daughter."

"Really, Mom?"

"Yes, Ginni, really. We were best friends."

"Wow, Mom." I'm fascinated. My mom is not a spiritual person and yet she's experienced something I've believed in but never been able to attain or experience.

"I've done this before and it was a lot of fun, and it's going to be even more fun this time."

I know she means dying, but before I can ask she turns and walks out of the kitchen escorted by Sophie and Sunny, two yellow furry bookends on either side of her. The girls spend more and more of their time with her, but still sleep with me.

I walk back to my room, hop on my bed, grab my journal off the nightstand, and write:

She is very old now. Until recently her blue eyes sparkled,
but the strokes have taken away not only the glow, but
also the shape.
Her mind is foggy more than clear, yet within that fog
is a clarity
about life and love and hope
that was never there before.
She has become an amazing and remarkable teacher.

A woman who never believed in God
or heaven
or angels
or spirits,
is being visited by those she loved
who ceased walking this earthly existence
long ago.

Never a believer,
and one who lived in fear,
She now speaks of the imminent end of her life
as something she has done before
that was a lot of fun
Something she says this time
Will be even more fun.

She's reminiscing about her life
Not just the current one
but the one that came before
A time when we were not
Mother and daughter
but still held together
by a bond so strong
that we became united in this life
in a relationship
filled with complexity
and challenge
and more love
than one could ever imagine

—Dr. Virginia A. Simpson
March 25, 2004

Chapter 17:

Oxygen Wars

To breathe or not to breathe, that is the question
—Virginia A. Simpson

MAY 2004

Although we are no longer in a crisis, we have not returned to where we were just a few months ago. Mom remains a mere flicker of who she once was, and our candles no longer burn bright.

I wish our lives could return to the way they once were. She's almost ninety years old, yet I still hope that since she's sprung back before, she can do it again. Hope doesn't die with ease or all at once. Rather, it is chipped away until nothing is left but dust and tears.

We are both in a new and perilous world and doing the best we can as we stumble through our days. I'm still competent at work. I continue to lead groups, supervise volunteers, write grants and newsletters, give speeches, and appear on radio and television. At home, I am a neophyte, yet the leader. If I fail, I don't trust Peter will be there to pick up the pieces of my mother's life. I never ask him for help because I'm certain he wouldn't, based on his actions when Mom went into the hospital and after she'd had the life-threatening procedure. He's visited her twice and offered no assistance in the five years she's been here. Mom's niece, my New York cousin Dona, has visited a number of times since Mom came to live with me. During her first visit, while Mom was napping, Dona said, "Your brother feels his mother was kidnapped." I said nothing, but later wished I'd replied, "And you believe him?"

I've lost confidence in Dr. Dillon, and I'm not so sure about Mom's internist, Dr. Mary. Neither doctor listens to me, nor do they address my concerns when I tell them Mom looks worse, and I see so little improvement in her cognitive functions that I don't believe the Aricept works. Dr. Dillon's exams are cursory at best, and he's dismissive when I ask questions or suggest he order a CAT scan or MRI. I took her to see Dr. Mary, but when she did little more than listen to Mom's chest and defend Dr. Dillon's competence, I knew it was time we found another doctor.

As Mom becomes frailer and her health declines, I grow stronger, focused, and more determined to ensure she gets the best possible healthcare. Her once reddish skin is now ashy, pale with gray undertones. She's lost weight and all interest in everything she loved—reading, current events, politics, and playing bridge. She no longer reads while she eats, and the newspaper remains pristine, the crossword puzzle squares left empty. She always napped but now the naps stretch out for hours.

My mother has turned into a passive witness to her own precarious life, her welfare dependent on the choices I must make for

124 THE SPACE BETWEEN

her. I am no longer willing to defer to doctors just because they have medical degrees.

I ask around, and more than one person recommends Dr. Theresa Sanders. A week later Mom and I sit in silence as we wait for her in an examination room. Dr. Sanders, a lean, dark-haired woman, sweeps into the high-ceilinged room, which is light, bright, and cheery despite being interior with no windows. She strides over to Mom, introduces herself, and removes the stethoscope draped around her neck.

"Let me listen to your heart, Mrs. Simpson." She puts her stethoscope to Mom's chest and asks her to take a deep breath. And then another. And another as she moves around to Mom's back. I breathe in sync with Mom's inhales and exhales. Her wheeze is apparent.

Dr. Sanders tosses the stethoscope on the counter, writes something on a chart, then pivots in Mom's direction. "I suspect you have congestive heart failure and your oxygen intake is insufficient. I'm going to do a quick test."

I sit still in my chair like a child told not to move and watch the doctor for any sign of concern. Her face is blank. So is mine. The back of my neck is hot and moist. The room is cool.

Dr. Sanders opens a drawer and takes out a clip, and as she clamps it on Mom's finger, Mom says, "What's that?"

"This clip shines light through one side of your finger while a detector measures the light that comes through the other side. This will give us a good guess about how much oxygen you're getting with each breath, because blood cells saturated with oxygen trap and reflect light differently than those that don't."

The test is brief.

"You're not getting enough oxygen." She picks up the receiver of the beige phone on the wall. "Leslie, I want you to order oxygen tanks and have them delivered to Mrs. Simpson's home today." She turns her attention to me and says, "What's your address?" I tell her and she repeats it into the phone.

Two hours later, the doorbell rings, and after I pull an unwilling Sunny and Sophie into the backyard, I open the front door. A large man with a scruffy red beard and tawny, long hair pulled back in a ponytail says, "Simpson residence?"

"Yes."

"I'm Don and I'm here with the equipment ordered by Dr. Sanders."

It takes two trips for him to bring in the caravan of equipment consisting of two large green cylinders of oxygen, plastic bags, a two-wheel cart, and a large gray contraption. Each item is like a heavy boulder thrown on my chest, and the only thing that stops me from sinking is that I'm not in water. Mom pretends to watch TV from her perch on the couch but I catch her sneaking quick looks at the whole coffle.

"Where do you want me to put everything?"

"I'm not sure what everything is," I say with a shrug.

"Okay, I'll tell you." He gestures to the large green tanks, one of which rests on the cart. "This is a mobile oxygen tank for use during the day." He tears open one of the plastic bags and pulls out what looks like a small metal tube with a compass on it. "This is a regulator. It controls the level of oxygen that comes out of the tank." He affixes it to the tank with a flat green piece with different size holes and uses it like a wrench to tighten the regulator. He then rips open another bag that contains plastic tubes. He attaches one end to the tank then wheels the tank over to my mother.

"Mrs. Simpson?"

"Yes," she says with raised eyebrows as she shifts her body towards him.

"This is a nasal cannula."

"So."

He explains what he's going to do, then hooks the tube around Mom's ears and puts the end with two prongs into her nostrils.

Mom reacts with a jolt.

I'm surprised and dubious about Mom's reaction. I was given oxygen in an ambulance ride to the hospital after a rollover accident on Interstate 10 in 1995 and welcomed the gentle, cool airflow, so I know the experience isn't harsh.

"Can you feel the air coming into your nose?"

"Yes," she almost hisses. "How long do I have to wear this thing?" Her lip curls in a sneer.

"All the time."

"All the time? Even when I shower?"

"You can take it off to shower." He nods and smiles.

"Well that's a relief," she says without a hint of sincerity, and turns her attention back to the TV.

Don shows me how to read the regulator to make certain it's set for the right airflow and also so I'll know when it's time to change tanks.

With every word he says I get more anxious. My mother's life, her very breath, depends on me. *What if I forget how to hook up her tank? What if I don't know how to read the regulator or it falls off or something else goes wrong?* There's no one I can rely on, other than Bob during our evening conversations, but he's in Texas and I'm in California. I'm grateful that he plans to visit next week, but right now I'm alone and the burden feels too heavy.

I'm too small for this. I don't want to be an adult. I want to turn around and find someone else who will take over for me. I will myself to be strong for Mom. I wear a mask of competence and don't let my discomfort show. I pretend I'm okay and soon I'm on autopilot and my concerns and fears have been buried alive.

"Where do you want me to put this?" Don gestures to the gray piece of equipment, which is two or three feet high and almost as wide.

"What is it?"

"This is an oxygen concentrator. She'll need this when she's in bed or sleeping. It has to be plugged in, so you'll want it near an outlet."

I take him to Mom's room but can't find an outlet that isn't in use so we put the concentrator in the bathroom. He attaches a cannula with longer tubing to the concentrator so that it will stretch into Mom's room. He explains how everything works and warns me that an alarm will ring if it stops providing the oxygen to Mom. "But that shouldn't happen, so don't worry."

Telling me not to worry is like asking ice cream not to melt in the sun.

⌣

Mom never comes right out and says she hates the cannula and oxygen tank. She doesn't have to.

Later that night, after I let the dogs out and they've come back in, I stop at Mom's room to see how she's doing. She lies on her side facing away from the door, and the cannula is next to her.

"Mom!" I sound like I'm scolding a small, naughty child. "What is that"—I point—"doing on your bed instead of in your nose?"

She rolls over and sits up with her back against the wicker headboard.

"I don't like it," she says and crosses her arms.

I huff, spread my legs like a cowboy ready for a gunfight, and put my hands on my hips. "Mom, you have to wear it. You're not getting enough oxygen." I wait for her to react and when she doesn't, I say, "Put it on." I'm stunned to hear my mother's voice come out of my mouth.

She sighs, tsks, waggles her head, and looks at me with an expression that would make a snake weep. She grasps the tube like it's repulsive, pulls it over her ears, and puts the cannula into her nostrils. "There! Are you satisfied?"

"I can think of things that would be more satisfying, but yes, Mom, I'm satisfied."

Mom almost smiles and I put my fist to my mouth to stifle a chuckle.

"Thank you," I say in a soft voice as I lean in and kiss her cheek before I head back to my room. I can't wait to call Bob and melt into the gentle comfort of his voice.

———

Within a few days, my mother has returned to normal and doesn't show signs of dementia. She reads the newspaper, discusses current events, wants to play cards, and reads her ever-present paperback book while she eats. I'm pissed that Dr. Dillon never considered that my mother's cognitive decline was due to lack of oxygen to her brain and not dementia. He wasted our time and months of Mom's life. I take her off the Aricept, certain that she never needed to be on it. To my delight and relief, she continues to improve. She says nothing to make me think she is aware she has been gone for a while, and I never mention it because I don't want to say anything to cause her discomfort or scare her. I'm just happy to have her back.

Happy—except that every day we fight over the oxygen. She hates it and pulls the cannula out of her nose, and I tell her to put it back in. Every day, morning, noon, and night, we go through the same battle, and my level of frustration and irritation rises. I stomp around the house and mutter to myself as I attempt not to fly off the proverbial handle.

Two weeks of this, and I can't tolerate the constant agitation and disruption. I don't want to police my mother. I'm tired of being angry, and I'm ready to explode.

I find her in the family room watching *Wheel of Fortune* on the TV. Her tank is with her but the cannula lies next to her on the couch. Sunny and Sophie are splayed out on the floor nearby.

I've had it, but instead of fighting with her to put the damn thing back in, I say, in a steady and firm voice: "Mom."

Sunny and Sophie jump up, run to my side, and nuzzle and lick my hands. My two pet therapists attempt to bring down the heat of my emotions—or maybe they think I'm mad at them, and unlike people, who close off, they move closer in love to calm the storm.

Mom turns away from the TV, lowers the volume, and stares at me.

"I'm not going to argue with you about this anymore," I say and nod towards the lifeless tube at her side.

"Well that's a relief," she says and picks up the remote control.

Before she can turn the volume up, I say, "Mom! You have three choices." I bite my lip and pause for a moment. "You can wear the oxygen with a bad attitude . . . You can wear the oxygen with a good attitude . . . Or you can not wear the oxygen and die. It's your choice."

She sits frozen for a moment. Her brows are so tight they almost look like one thin pencil line. She grabs the tube and places it into her nostrils, and is never again without her oxygen except when she showers. And to my surprise, she wears it with a good attitude. She doesn't complain, she makes no faces, and she says nothing negative about the intrusion of this ugly, uncomfortable, cumbersome appendage into her life.

Once I know she's getting enough air, I can breathe without tension. At least for the moment.

⸻

Since the first time I saw a therapist in 1969, I've thought of myself as someone in touch with her feelings. I seem to have forgotten that when a person is under significant stress over a prolonged period of time, the body floods with chemicals, becomes overwhelmed, and systems begin to shut down. I knew I was tired, but I lost touch, or perhaps never got in touch, with the erosion and exhaustion coping with Mom has on me. I move by rote through each day anxious, short-tempered, on high alert, and edgy, but I don't recognize within myself all the signs of burnout that I teach my volunteers. I'm not in full burnout yet, but I am on the downward slide.

I believe I'm doing just "*fine.*" I forgot to remember what a retired Catholic nun with an Irish brogue said during a hospice training. "'Fine' sometimes means: **F**ucked Up, **I**nsecure, **N**eurotic, and **E**motional."

So if you ask me how I am and I respond, "Fine," keep that in mind.

Chapter 18:

When Yesterday Becomes Today

The past is never dead. It's not even past.
—William Faulkner, *Requiem for a Nun,* 1951

Angry is just sad's bodyguard.
—Liza Palmer

Nothing ever goes away until it teaches us what we need to know.
—Pema Chodron

JUNE 2004

Mom's a new person since she opted to wear the oxygen with a good attitude. She doesn't complain, and our lives smooth into routine days with any conflict tucked away. We are back to being friends and discuss everything from the upcoming presidential election to stories about her card-playing girlfriends.

As I relax into enjoying Mom more as the good friend she had become before she moved in, I neglect to keep in mind that I never know what a new day with my mother may bring. It would be too hard to move through each day scared about her health or waiting for our next conflict. It's human nature to live as though nothing will go wrong; otherwise we'd all be paralyzed wrecks as we waited for the next natural disaster, terrorist attack, accident, or interpersonal conflict.

I work from home as often as possible on days Mom doesn't play cards. It's not always convenient, because it means running back and forth to the Center to get the mail or meet with a parent who wants to bring their child, or sometimes to meet with an officer from a foundation who needs to see for him- or herself that we are who we purport to be. I don't schedule appointments on Thursdays because this is the day I chauffeur Mom to her nail and hair appointments. I don't resent doing this but I feel pulled between the desire to ensure my organization lasts and the need to make sure Mom is taken care of. I help Mom and the cumbersome oxygen tank out of the car, then walk with them to her first appointment. I stop in to say hello, pay for her services, and wait until she is settled before I leave for my office. Once there, I check the mail and return phone calls until I pick Mom up an hour later and treat her to lunch. Today we stop at Sammy's, where we share our favorite Messy Sundae.

It's midafternoon and I sit at my desk, deep in thought and focused on the computer screen as I struggle to find the right words to entice a charitable foundation to fund my dream of a grief camp for children. The room is cool and the house silent. Sophie and Sunny are at the groomer's. Mom naps in her room at the other side of the house.

The unexpected touch of Mom's hand on my shoulder as she says my name startles me, and I skyrocket out of the chair with a scream. My heart beats at a speed that would leave the Jamaican sprinter Usain Bolt in the dust.

"I'm sorry, Ginni, I'm sorry," Mom says, her brows ruffled and raised.

I blurt out my first thought. "See what your son did to me?" I punctuate each word like a hammer.

We freeze for a minute, face-to-face, each of us with a hand over our hearts like we're about to say the Pledge of Allegiance.

We stand there for a few moments, trying to find some way back to equilibrium. Mom's eyes have the scared look of an innocent child who has no idea what happened and doesn't know what to do other than hold still and wait for directions. Once my breath is normal and the internal storm has dissipated, I suggest we go to the family room, where we can sit and discuss the situation.

I escort Mom to the couch, then stop at the kitchen and pour her a glass of her favorite cranberry raspberry drink and water for me. I hand her the juice before I settle in close to her. I want—no, I need—her to understand why I reacted like a fawn hunted by a lion.

"Mom, I have an exaggerated startle response, which means I overreact to any unanticipated sound or touch. I don't choose to react this way. I would prefer to be calm. But once I'm frightened, my body doesn't return to normal like most people's because of all the times your precious Peter jumped from out of nowhere and scared me before he'd twist my arm behind my back, tickle me until it hurt, or hit me."

"Henry hit me when I was a child," Mom says. Her eyes shift up and to the left as though she views something distant. "When I'd tell my mother he hit me, she'd say, 'Oh, no, my Henry would never do that.'" Henry was my mother's older brother. She always turns the conversation into one about Henry and herself whenever I say anything about Peter.

"Mom, I'm still scared of Peter."

"I'll tell you the truth, Ginni, sometimes I am too."

At first her admission is a surprise, but then I remember what I witnessed when I was twelve or thirteen. I was in the kitchen and I walked in slow steps towards the dining room, pulled towards the door by loud voices. I pushed the swinging door open a smidge and trembled. Peter loomed large over our tiny mother like a malignant dark thundercloud. I froze, stopped by fear that Peter was going to hit her. He stared at Mom with the scary, odd expression in his eyes he always had in the last moments before he would explode into a flurry of slaps and fists on my body. This had been going on ever since I was a very little girl, and my mother and father never knew because Peter threatened to hurt me worse if I told, and I believed him. Peter didn't hit Mom, but in that instant I was certain she was in grave danger and couldn't protect either of us. Still, I held a fantasy until I was nineteen that if she knew what he did to me, and she had the power, she would have protected me.

"So, Mom, if Henry did this to you and you know how resentful you were that your mother defended him, how come you do the same thing to me?"

She leans her elbows on her knees and begins to wring her hands, then looks up at me with a flat, empty gaze. "I don't know, Ginni. I'm sorry. I wish I could tell you but I honestly don't know," she says, and her voice trails off into a solemn whisper.

Even though her response doesn't clear up the mystery of her actions, I don't push further, because I can tell by how she looks and sounds that she did her best to explain and doesn't know the answer. Still, I'm frustrated, because I'm left to never understand actions that hurt me and too often drove a wedge between my mom and me.

———

A week later, I'm at the kitchen sink about to take my last sip of coffee. Mom watches me from the other side of the island. Often when I stand at the sink, I'll turn around and Mom will be staring at me like she is now. I hate that she watches me. I wish I understood why this bothers me, because I realize that one day she won't be there when I turn around, and I'll more than miss her and regret every time I felt annoyed.

"Ginni, Peter and Ellyn want to come visit. I can't drive, so can they come here?"

Although my stomach feels like I just ate a handful of jumping beans, I manage to keep my voice neutral. "I'll have to think about it, Mom, but the truth is, I don't want them in my house."

"I don't know why you hate him so much." Mom's voice is harsh.

I spin around and glare at Mom, a sneer on my face in spite of myself. "You can't understand?! You can't understand," I shriek. "How many times do I have to tell you what Peter did and how many times will you forget?"

I'm loud and must seem angry to Mom, but the truth is I am frustrated and feel invisible. I sink inside myself like a turtle pulled into its shell. I'm no longer fifty-four years old. I'm nineteen. I don't respond with the emotional intelligence of an educated and trained professional who helps others cope with their emotions. Instead, I act like an outraged teenage girl.

In this moment, I'm reliving everything I felt in 1968.

I don't want to tell these stories but there's no other way to explain why I reacted this way or why the spaces and awkwardness exist between my mother and me.

⁓

In September 1968, Peter and I argued about me selling him my Volkswagen. I'd bought the car with my own money when I was seventeen and didn't want it anymore. The argument started on the phone when Peter told me he'd sold his car for $790, which was ten dollars less than the $800 he was paying for my car. When he said he wanted Mom to pay for the ad he'd placed in the newspaper to sell his car, I was disgusted that he would take advantage of her that way. I said I wouldn't sell him my car if he insisted Mom pay. His threatening words, "You better," were followed by "I'm coming over," and the slam of the phone.

A few minutes later, I was seated at the kitchen banquette with my girlfriend Margaret, sipping a glass of ice water, when I heard the front door open.

Peter burst into the kitchen, followed by his wife, Rachel. He loomed over me. "You better sell me your car." His eyes narrowed into a scowl and his mouth clenched.

"I won't if you're going to charge Mom. You're getting my car for what amounts to ten dollars. How can you be so cheap?"

"You're going to sell me that car," he yelled as he swept my glass off the table toward my face. I ducked and the glass shattered against the wall behind my head, leaving me wet and sprinkled with glass shards.

I should have known from previous fights with him that the only way to remain safe was to stay quiet, but I had a hot little temper and ignored the tightening in my stomach. I didn't stop to think or I would have realized I was on a dangerous precipice. I screamed, "Now for sure I'll never sell you my car."

"You better," he yelled, and before I knew it, he kicked my arm. I jumped out of my seat, hurling every swear word I knew at him, too angry to notice the intense pain in my arm. I saw Margaret slip out of the kitchen after the first blow and heard the front door slam as she left. Peter's wife stayed. I had no idea what Peter would do next. I was in danger, and the only thing I could think about was finding my escape route.

I ran toward the porch that led to the back door. Peter came after me. When he reached me, I folded into myself to protect my body as he kicked my arm again and again. I must have shouted—I don't know if I was crying—but he wouldn't stop. I knew from past experience that if I fought back, he would escalate his assault. Rachel pulled him away for a moment, but before I had a chance to run, he broke free and charged towards me. Even if I'd been able to get out through the back door, I had no real chance to escape to safety. He always caught me when I'd run away during our fights after Dad died.

He cornered me as I reached the service porch door and continued his assault. As though a switch were turned off, every thought and sensation in my body froze and I crumpled to the floor in a fetal position. I was trapped and too scared to move. In the animal kingdom, predators sometimes leave weak or dead prey alone. I wasn't so fortunate.

Peter continued to yell and kick until Rachel pulled him off again. I had no chance to move before he returned and kicked me harder than before. I'll never forget the sight of his huge shoe pulled back like a gun being cocked and then released into my arm.

Rachel reached us, looking angrier than I'd ever seen her. She kept screaming at Peter. I heard the sound but I couldn't understand anything she said. Somehow, she convinced him to stop and they left.

For a few minutes I cowered in the corner, alone, wounded, and in shock. I pulled myself up and stumbled into the kitchen, crying and screaming to the empty house. Every inch of my arm throbbed with intense pain.

Mom's key clicked in the front door and as soon as she entered the kitchen, I did my best to calm my sobs so I could speak. I pointed to my bruised arm and cried, "Look what Peter did to me! Don't sell him my car! I don't want him to have my car." My car was registered in Mom's name, so she had to sign the pink slip to release ownership. I was certain she would agree with me.

I was more than stunned when, instead of sympathizing with gentle words, she said in a neutral tone, "I have to call Peter and Rachel to find out what happened." She turned away from me and left me alone in the kitchen, where I stood shocked and immobilized.

A few minutes later, her high heels clicked across the linoleum floor. Mom stopped in front of me and put her hands on her hips. "Rachel says you didn't talk nice to Petey."

"I don't care how I talked him," I roared as I waved my one good arm. "No one deserves what he did to me. Don't sell him my car! I don't want him to have my car." My voice trailed off into a whimper, but that evening I kept repeating my plea not to let him have my car.

The next day, despite my demands and injuries, and without talking to me, Mom sold Peter my car, gave him ten dollars for his ad, and even threw in a brand new sunroof. It seemed the height of injustice that someone who had violently injured me should be given a gift, especially by our mother.

Her actions hurt me worse than any of Peter's kicks. Not only did she discount my wishes, she rewarded him for hitting me. As I thought about what she had done, I realized how much I missed my father and thought of all the times Mom had said, "You're lucky it wasn't me who died." Some luck. My daddy would have protected me, but there was nothing I could do now. I didn't tell her how betrayed I felt, because I had no words for what I was feeling. I was convinced that nothing I could say would matter to her. I knew that Peter meant more to her than I did—she had proved it again and again.

For the next two weeks, my bruised and useless right arm reminded me how painful and ineffective my presence in this world had become. The bruises eventually healed, but my mother's betrayal never did. I felt abandoned and alone, certain that no one in the world loved me. I'd been stripped of my power, and for as long as I lived in that house, I felt like a rat trapped in a maze, afraid Peter might attack.

In 1985, seventeen years after this encounter with Peter, we found out that he had hit Ellyn, his wife of one year, then made a half-assed, sure-to-fail suicide attempt and institutionalized himself. I happened to be in Los Angeles a few days later, visiting my mother. She told me the story soon after I arrived as we sat together on the couch in my childhood den, the place where Mom would read to me when I was a little girl. When I heard that Peter was still violent, I wanted to return to my home in Mountain View, California, and get as far away from him as possible.

"I've got to go see him now and I want you to come with me."

"No, Mom," I said with a frown.

"What do you mean, 'no'?"

"I mean I can't, Mom. I'm afraid of him," I said, my voice low and firm, trying to give no indication of weakness. I thought if I sounded strong, she'd accept my refusal.

"How can you not visit your brother when he is going through such a terrible time and needs his family?" Her mouth twisted and she looked at me with hard, cold eyes, as if to say I was the lowest scum in the world for not wanting to visit her son. Something inside me shriveled. I was pierced by a familiar, ancient guilt, triggered by her need for me to submit to her wishes when it came to Peter. Soon I was filled with self-loathing, and found myself agreeing with Mom's harsh belief that I was unkind and not compassionate enough. I thought that what I'd learned in therapy taught me that guilt is a useless emotion, but the lesson stood no chance against my mother's hostile glare, a look that should have been reserved for a mass murderer. All the fight in me was gone, and I believed I had no choice but to go with her to see him.

I accompanied Mom like a prisoner, dead woman walking, trapped in the car on the way to my own execution. After we arrived, a receptionist made a call and then buzzed us inside, where we sat on uncomfortable chairs while we waited. When Peter entered wearing gray scrubs, Mom rose and walked over to him. She reached up and he bent to hug her. I fought the urge to throw up. After they sat down to visit for a few minutes, Mom said, "I'll leave you two alone." She ignored my sad, scared eyes, which were begging her to stay. I stayed because I was already imprisoned by the guilt and shame from our previous conversation.

Peter led me to another room, where we sat down on hard metal chairs facing each other about a foot apart—close enough to smell his noxious sweat. I watched Peter's face as he shared what he'd done to Ellyn and how much he regretted hitting her.

As he kept talking, his eyes had the same wild, maniacal expression I'd seen too many times right before he'd lose control and hit me.

One thing saved me—I'd learned basic active listening during my training to counsel dying and grieving people. When Peter said, "I regret hitting her," I responded with my most soft-eyed, sincere look of compassion. "So, you regret hitting her." I utilized every skill I could muster to stay calm no matter what he said.

When Mom rejoined us in what seemed like eons later, I excused myself and headed to the ladies room. Once I was alone and safe, tears cascaded down my cheeks and I trembled like a frightened puppy. I paced the length of the small room, talking to myself as I stomped past stalls and sinks. When I calmed down, I washed my face and wiped away the tears. I said into the mirror, "How could you do this, Mom? How could you put me at risk?" I grabbed a paper towel, dried my face, stood tall, and marched out to say good-bye to Peter.

I drove back to Mountain View the next day, sometimes crying and sometimes screaming at my mother, who was still at her home.

She had chosen Peter over me—again.

Now she wants him to enter my home. *Why do you hate him?* my mother asks. I don't hate him. I'm still terrified of him, and the thought of him coming here all these years later tightens around me like a vise.

I don't want him here, but he needs to see his mother and my mother needs to see her son. I still have to reconcile doing the right thing despite our unresolved past.

With all the therapy, education, yoga, meditation retreats, and reading a bazillion psychology and self-help books, you'd think by now I would have healed the old wounds for good. Several times I believed I had let this issue go, but it snakes back in, an unwanted guest.

I thought I'd forgiven him, but that was when the "problem," my mother, didn't live in my home, and when the person who had hurt me was out of my life so completely that I didn't have to hear his name. But when my biggest nightmare will find out where I live and invade my home, hard emotions reawaken like Rip Van Winkle after his hundred-year sleep. Forgiving her seems impossible to imagine, but with my mother closing in on the end of her life, and the deadline for me to heal our relationship near, I need to find a way to wrestle with this wound that holds our love hostage and separates our hearts.

Although I will never forget what happened with Peter and my mother, and I'll always be afraid of him because he's never acknowledged or apologized for his violence, the important thing now is how I react today and the choices I make.

———

The next day, I tell Mom it's okay for Peter and Ellyn to come. Mom responds with a cool "thank you," and says she'll let them know. That evening she tells me they'll arrive around noon a week from Saturday and leave by two. I won't stop them from entering my house, but I want to make sure they can't search through my personal items and papers. When Bob arrives that week, I ask him to install locks on my office and bedroom doors. We leave the house to go see a movie before Peter and Ellyn arrive. I call Mom before we return home to see if they have gone.

I find no solace in having done the right thing in regards to his visit because once again I gave up part of myself for Mom. I'm disappointed in myself for acting like a grumpy child with a bad attitude. While this self-judgment may seem harsh, it is the best I can do.

Chapter 19:

Little Girl Ninety

Age merely shows what children we remain.
—Johann Wolfgang von Goethe

AUGUST 28, 2004

Mom is ninety years old today. Our lives returned to normal after Peter's visit, although I'm not sure you could call a small old woman tethered to a large oxygen tank living in her middle-aged daughter's home anything resembling normal. Still, now that I don't have to hear or think about Peter, he is no longer a source of conflict and our lives are mild—mild in the same sense that 107 degrees in the desert during August is considered pleasant and warm.

Mom and I are both August babies, but I'm a Leo and she's a Virgo, which as far as I can tell simply means she's neater and more organized than me.

We have never made a big deal out of birthdays. The only time Mom had a birthday party for me was when I was five years old. I never thought I'd missed out on anything until I was an adult and watched with wonder as my friends created special birthday parties for their children.

On my birthday morning, August 12th, as soon as I enter the kitchen, Sunny and Sophie leave their posts as my sentries and rush over to Mom, still in her pale blue cotton pajamas seated at the kitchen desk. She pets the girls for a moment then turns towards toward me. "Happy Birthday, Ginni." She nudges a folded piece of steno pad paper into my hand. Her voice is fragile and sad as she says, "I'm sorry, Ginni. I'm sorry I couldn't get you a card."

"That's okay, Mom," I say with my voice upbeat, as though this will lift her spirits and make her feel better.

Silently, I read her note:

Dearest Ginni:
August 12th 55 years ago I got lucky.
You were born. I've loved you ever since.
To me you are very special. You're everything I hoped for.
Your [sic] beautiful, smart, thoughtful, Kind.
My spelling was never too good but my thoughts are.
Your Mother
(love you)
(very much)

I shake my head and snort a little chuckle at her signature. She always signs "Your Mother," as though if she didn't, I might think someone else's mother wrote to me.

"Mom, you couldn't have given me anything better." I smile at her.

"You mean it?" She tilts her head and looks up at me with a sadness in her eyes that tells me she wants to believe me but wishes she could have done more.

"Yes, Mom, of course I do." I hug her and kiss her cheek. "I love you," I assure her with a nod and cheerful smile. Sunny and Sophie jostle us with enthusiastic tail wags. Soon we're hot in our affectionate hug and have to let go.

As a gift to myself, I hired someone to take care of Mom and the girls so that later that morning I can fly to Dallas to celebrate my birthday with Bob. I want our time together to be carefree, but there's no such thing anymore. Mom is never far from my thoughts, and I call her two or three times a day while I'm away. Even so, I grasp on to these few days of relative peace and quiet, enjoying getting to know Bob better, laughing, and falling more in love as we spend our days touring Dallas or playing golf. We enjoy our evenings visiting with his friends or alone doing simple things like cooking dinner together and watching TV while he holds me in his arms.

———

When I get back, it's time to figure out what to do for Mom's birthday. I didn't plan a party for her ninetieth because most of her friends are dead and the few still alive live far away. Although she plays Pan with a group of ladies at the senior center every week, she doesn't consider any of them her friends. They have nothing in common except cards.

Earlier this year, one night when she came home after a card game, she dropped her keys on the kitchen counter, shook her head, and sniffed, "These women. We were talking about sex and one said she'd never had oral sex and thought it was disgusting."

Mom stood straight and added with an imperious tone, "And I said to her, 'Well, if you haven't had oral sex then you've never had sex.'" Mom waved her hand in dismissal. "Tsk. They're such prudes."

My mind reeled at this woman disguised as my mother voluntarily discussing sex with me—this was the first time. I thought back to when I was seventeen. Mom was standing at the sink washing dishes. I said, "Mom, why can't you talk about s-e-x with me?"

She turned toward me, her face flushed red, and stammered, "I—I—I don't know, Ginni." She never stammered or blushed, but the mere mention of the word *sex* seemed to unnerve her. I laughed inside because I had a secret: I knew all about sex and was no longer a virgin. I was the stereotypical, smug, teenage know-it-all girl and I was toying with my Mom when I asked her about sex. That was thirty-eight years ago, and now, at almost ninety, she's complaining about card-playing friends who are prudes. What a difference. I look at her again, just to make sure that these words came out of my mother's mouth, and chuckle to myself. It's never too late to be surprised.

―――

"Happy birthday, Mom," I say with the enthusiasm of a cheer-leader as I enter the kitchen on the morning of her ninetieth birthday. She's already made coffee and is sitting at her usual spot in the kitchen on a secretarial chair where she reads *The Los Angeles Times* and *The Desert Sun* every morning. She puts *The Times* down and reaches her hand up to cradle my head as I bend to kiss her cool cheek.

I pull the wrapped gift from behind my back and hand it to her.

"What's this?" she says with a half smile and wide eyes. She knows what it is, because every year I give her pajamas; the only surprise is what they'll look like.

Mom slides the envelope with the card out from beneath the ribbon, slips her finger under the flap, and tears it open. She reads in silence, glances up at me, her cerulean eyes soft with love, and looks back down at the card. She reads me what I wrote. I hold my hand up to stop her. "You can stop, Mom. I know what I wrote. I don't have to hear it."

I don't know why hearing my words makes me uncomfortable, but it does. I wish I'd allowed her to keep reading. After her death, when I look back at this precious time, I can see that my words touched something deep inside her, and she wanted me to hear that I'd written she was a wonderful mother and I loved her very much. I missed the opportunity for a moment of gentle kindness, a moment I can never get back.

She pulls the ribbon off, jiggles the top loose, and parts the tissue. She pulls out the shiny pink Natori pajamas with powder blue piping and holds the top up to her chest. "They're beautiful," she says, and I beam in response.

"They're silky on the outside and flannel on the inside to keep you warm."

"It's not exactly cold, Ginni," Mom says, and we both laugh because it's summer, with days spicy hot enough to boil your skin off.

"I know, Mom, but it won't always be hot."

Mom plays Pan on her ninetieth birthday. The ladies she plays cards with at the Joslyn Senior Center plan to surprise her with a cake, and asked me to come inside when I pick her up that afternoon.

Mom smiles like a happy five-year-old as the cake is brought in and everyone at the Center joins in to sing *Happy Birthday, Dear Ruth.* Mom inhales as deeply as she can, then blows what little breath she has at the candles. I lean in and, with as much subtlety as possible, blow with her to extinguish all the candles. Mom beams as everyone applauds. A staff member cuts the cake and passes it to the ladies. They eagerly eat it, then everyone seems to vanish from the room. No gifts. No great fanfare. No party favors or games or sharing of memories. As we depart the building and all the way home, Mom can't stop talking about "the beautiful party they threw for me."

I'm stunned. My mother is never thrilled about much of anything, and for her to be elated about nothing more than cake and ice cream rattles my brain. The cake wasn't even chocolate, her favorite.

———

I wasn't invited when Peter and his wife threw a party for Mom's eightieth birthday, but she never said much about it so I don't know if she was pleased or not. I've always felt that whatever I did was never enough. My gifts were greeted with nothing more than a tepid "Thank you." A good example is the VCR I gave her for her eightieth.

"So, Mom, how do you like the VCR?"

"I don't."

No explanation, just flat, hard, blunt words hurled at me over the phone. Even when she began to record all her shows so she'd never miss them, she didn't thank me for this piece of equipment that added pleasure to her life. Mom could be a faultfinder, and she did a good job of it back then.

Now she's ninety, and I'm still adjusting to how she's changed.

Is she delusional again? How could she call fifteen minutes of cake and ice cream a party? At first the tone in my head is critical, but as I think about it, I realize she's become the person I have wanted to be, the one I have meditated to be, gone to therapy to be—someone who can find joy and gratitude in the smallest of gestures and events. If she is delusional, she's in the middle of a wondrous dream. I hope I don't have to wait another thirty-five years to find this Neverland she's entered.

That evening I take her to Don Diego's, the neighborhood Mexican restaurant that is one of our favorites. I don't even balk when she asks for a glass of wine. Most of the time I try to stop her from having a drink because I'm afraid she'll turn back into the mean alcoholic I remember too well. But she's in a good mood and it's her birthday. I'm certain this will be her last, even though we haven't talked about it and her doctor has never said the words "she's dying."

I know this is gradually happening, though I don't dare to whisper it aloud to myself or anyone else. It's in my bones, but I don't let on. I'm her daughter, so I'm good at hiding the tears that weigh on my heart.

I tell our waiter it's Mom's ninetieth birthday. Within a few moments, the owner and all the waiters come over to our table to wish her happy birthday, and one throws a huge sombrero on Mom's head. I wait for her to get upset and toss it off, but she smiles and laughs. My mother is never silly but tonight she is, and I adore this joyful little ninety-year-old girl.

"Hold still, Mom. I want to take a picture."

"Oh, no," she says. "I hate pictures."

"You look so cute."

"Okay, okay. Let me take this thing out," she says as she pulls the cannula out of her nose.

When I raise my camera, she puts her hand on her chest and laughs, and I take one of the few photographs of my mother smiling.

Today is the first time I've seen this side of my mother, and I wonder if I've captured a snapshot of the little girl she was when she was an innocent and sweet five-year-old child who went to the library, checked out five books, read most of them as she walked home, and couldn't wait to tell her mother all about them.

Chapter 20:

Conversations

But better to get hurt by the truth than comforted with a lie.

—Khaled Hosseini

NOVEMBER 8–11, 2004

We're on the wrong end of a battle that we can't win. The bright warm days, comfortable nights, and streets filled with happy tourists mock the emptiness inside our home. Since Mom's birthday, she has seemed deflated, like one of those day-after party balloons. Even with the oxygen to ease her labored breathing and keep her mind intact, something intangible is seeping away from her—and from me. Taking care of her feels like trying to push a boulder up a hill of loose rocks. Sometimes I think, *What's next?* I feel my own breath catch and I wonder if I have enough air to keep pushing.

Our trek to her doctor every two weeks has become more arduous with each visit. Harder for Mom, because she has to expend her small reserve of energy, leaving her gasping for air by the time we reach the office, and painful for me, because I'm saddled with sadness and the overpowering sense that I'm losing the battle to keep her alive. Sometimes I'm so exhausted and weary I feel like I'm not going to be able to take one more step forward, as though my life is being sucked away as hers declines.

This Tuesday has been busy. After my weekly morning group with grieving teens at Raymond Cree Middle School in Palm Springs, I hurry to my office to meet with Carol, the hospice bereavement coordinator, to finalize our plans for a holiday candle lighting ceremony.

Carol and I met a few years ago when I was called to a private Catholic school because two students had lost their father. The school asked me to do presentations on grief for their classmates in the third and fourth grades. Carol, a striking, tall young woman in her late thirties, was at the school when I arrived and joined me in both classes. She stood nearby as I spoke to the children about loss and asked them to share their experiences. Carol listened more than she talked, but when she did, her comments added more insights to what I'd said. I was surprised that we worked together as if we'd been doing it for years. We immediately became friends.

Today, after our plans for the candle lighting are finished, Carol rises to leave. As I walk her to the door, I'm surprised to hear myself say, "My mother's health is worse." I stuff my hands into my pant pockets. "I'm not competent to cope with her health needs. Add to that her increasing demands for my time and attention . . ." My words trail off. I look down and shake away my tears, then look up at Carol. "I'm drained and overwhelmed."

"Ginni, you should get her into hospice," Carol says, her voice gentle yet matter-of-fact.

"I can't do that, Carol. I don't know if she has only six months to live." I fold my arms across my tight chest.

Carol leans closer and touches my arm. "Although Medicare policy dictates that in order to be covered, a patient should have a life expectancy of no more than six months, they won't deny care if she exceeds that time." Carol pauses, and with a hint of a smile adds, "No one can predict the exact time of death. You just need her doctor to say she has six months and put in an order to hospice."

"I didn't realize we could do this."

"Most people don't." Carol shakes her head. "Doctors won't tell patients or their families because they view death as the enemy and hospice as defeat. I've seen too many people fight for life beyond the time they should, only to be confronted with ever-worsening and frightening decay and one horrible medical crisis after another. They miss out on the opportunity to receive all the wonderful services hospice offers."

"Like what?"

"You'll never have to go to another doctor's appointment, your mother's medications will be delivered to your house, nurses will visit on a regular basis, plus you can utilize the opportunity for respite by requesting a volunteer sit with your mother while you go out. And none of this will cost you a cent."

I have believed in hospice since I first learned about Dame Cicely Saunders, the founder of the hospice movement. I liked the idea of a team to help a person at the end of their life, but until today I didn't know hospice was available while a person was still active. As soon as I moved to the desert, I volunteered at Desert Hospice and visited terminally ill people, either in their homes or in a special ward allocated to hospice at Desert Regional

Medical Center. I've seen people at the end of their lives, all gray, incoherent, and often unconscious, and not one of them looked like my mother, who is alert and mobile.

Being a caregiver is different than being on the professional side of things. I hadn't counted on the ways grief would intermingle and muddle my perceptions and reactions. Now that death is near and impacts every aspect of our lives, I realize nothing I've done—not my education, research, training, or volunteer work—has prepared me for the heartbreak and stress I feel as a powerless witness to my mother's decline.

I'm a realist and know Mom won't recover from COPD (Chronic Obstructive Pulmonary Disease), congestive heart failure, and emphysema. To enter hospice, we must agree to palliative care. Mom will be kept comfortable but no extraordinary actions will be taken to extend her life. Hospice means we choose quality of life over quantity. All of this is in alignment with the conversations Mom and I have had over the years regarding what she would want at the end of her life. Mom gave me a map to follow and that's what I'm doing, but I don't know if she remembers or even still agrees with the decisions we plotted out long ago.

In 1989, Mom was visiting me in Northern California. One night, as I sat on her bed, I broached the subject of advanced directives for healthcare and what Mom would want when she was near the end of her life. Mom was clear she wanted no extraordinary means used to keep her alive if there was no chance for quality of life or recovery. She liked the idea of hospice. I took the opportunity to ask, "Mom, if you were dying, would it be okay if I cried in front of you?" I wanted to know because Mom taught me not to cry and would never cry herself, but I'd found those early lessons useless against years of therapy, which opened me to expressing my feelings, including tears.

Mom didn't answer right away. Then, with a sparkle in her eyes and a smile, she surprised me. "Yes. I think I'd like that."

And now, all these years later, I'm so glad we had that important conversation well before we were at the edge of crisis.

———

"Hello," I call out as I enter the house. Before I can get past the service porch, I'm greeted by the enthusiastic tail-wagging duo of Sunny and Sophie.

Mom's "hello" is hard to hear over the TV. She's in her bedroom but I don't go in to see her.

The girls prance like "best-in-show" dogs as they escort me across the house to my bedroom. After I've had the chance to bolster my courage with some doggie love, I'm ready to talk to Mom. The girls accompany me as I trudge towards her bedroom.

Before I enter Mom's room, I hover at the doorway and watch her briefly. I need a moment to move past the weight of sorrow in my chest and throat. She's sitting up, wearing the shiny pale pink pajamas I bought for her birthday. She stares ahead at the TV and doesn't notice me in the doorway.

I tap on her door. She cranes her neck to look at me.

"Mom, I need to talk to you," I say, keeping myself calm. I hope she can't see the sadness in my heart.

"Oh?" she says.

I step into the room and sit at the end of her bed. Sunny and Sophie go over to Mom. She pats their heads in an abstract manner and eyes me with the intensity of a scientist examining a specimen under the lens of a microscope.

I clear my throat and, after a hard gulp, start to speak in a tone I hope comes off as loving, sincere, and persuasive. "Mom, I had a conversation today with a colleague and because of what she told me, I think next time we go to the doctor's, we should ask her to get you into hospice."

Her eyes open wide, and she looks like she will say something, but before she can speak, a flood of words pour from me. "I only want to do this so we can get better care for you. That's the only reason. To get you better care." I try to illustrate my sincerity with hand gestures and body language, hoping to assure her that I have her best interests in mind. I've always talked with my hands, but tonight it's as though they're magic wands that hold the power to get Mom to agree.

"Go on," she says. Her bland tone offers no encouragement that I should continue. She stops petting the girls, and they grunt as they lie down on the floor next to her.

"We won't have to go to the doctor's office anymore—and you know how difficult it is to sit in the waiting room for the long wait with all those sick people."

"I don't mind," she says, and shifts back and forth like she's trying to find a comfortable spot on the bed.

I am so focused on what I think we need to do that I don't allow myself to ponder those three words. Maybe Mom is telling me she doesn't want to believe she is close to the end of her life and if she allows hospice, she'll have to acknowledge this unpalatable reality. Perhaps I am missing an opportunity to get closer, to share our wants, desires, and even fears. I'll never know, because I charge ahead.

"Of course you do. You complain every time we go," I add as almost a tagline. "Nurses will come visit you, and we'll get help when we need it. We'll even be able to have someone give you massages if you want," I say in a tone tinged with desperation.

She maintains a sphinxlike silence, her face serious and inscrutable.

"Mom?" I want to get some kind of reaction from her.

"What do you want me to say, Ginni?"

"Are you okay with this, Mom?" My heart is pounding as I wait to hear her answer. I have to make sure she is willing to go along with the plan.

"If you say so, Ginni," she says with a shrug—then, in a lower voice, "I trust you. You always do the right thing."

"Are you sure?" I need her to approve, fully and without question. What if later she changes her mind, what if she blames me for abandoning her?

"Yes, Ginni, I'm sure." Her voice is soft and she looks back at the TV.

"Thank you." I feel a momentary burn in my chest, still wondering if this is the right thing. I shake the thought off and reassure myself we've made the best choice. I lean forward to hug her. "I love you, Mom," I manage to eke out.

"I love you too. Now if we're finished here, I'd like to watch my show," Mom says, and looks past me like I'm an apparition.

On Thursday that same week, we visit her doctor. We trek across the parking lot, into the building, up the elevator to the second floor, then into the doctor's large, cold waiting room. This journey is long and strenuous for Mom. She pants and presses her hand against her chest.

How did we get here? Me a middle-aged woman in a caravan

with my elderly mother and her oxygen entourage trailing into the doctor's waiting room. It seems like no more than a moment ago I was nine years old and Mom was young and we sprinted up the flight of stairs to the new toy store on Robertson Boulevard in Los Angeles near the library. The shop was narrow, with glass-encased counters on either side of an aisle. Shelves to the ceiling brimmed with toys and dolls. A lanky, brown-haired man behind the counter pulled out the latest doll from the shelf behind him. Barbie! I'd never seen such a beautiful doll. Although I wasn't one to ask for much and often turned down Mom's offers to buy me things, that day I pointed and said to her, "That's the one I want. Can I have her, Mommy?"

"We'll take it," she said, and paid the three dollars to the gentleman, who then handed me the box with my very own Barbie.

I'd give anything if I could return to those innocent moments with my healthy young mother who's now been replaced by an old woman destined to leave me. I've been afraid to lose her ever since my dad died, and now what I've dreaded most since I was twelve is my everyday, slap-in-the-face reality.

———

I scan the doctor's waiting room, locate the only seats available, and settle Mom in next to a woman with a wet, hacking cough. Once she's seated, I head over to the long bank of desks that straddle the width of this large, impersonal, white room to check her in. I want to get her out of this disease-filled place. They should have special waiting rooms for patients who are vulnerable like my mother. Every time I come here I worry she'll catch pneumonia and never recover.

We sit for longer than the usual forty-five minutes. Well,

Mom sits, her head buried in a paperback with a turquoise blue cover the same color as her eyes. *Bel Canto* by Ann Patchett. I'm like a jack-in-the-box. I pop up and charge to the front desk every fifteen minutes, where I keep telling the unimpressed receptionist how unsafe it is for my fragile, elderly mother to be forced to stay in a room with sick people. I do my best to keep my voice pleasant, but I hear sharp edges leach out with my words. My head swirls as I consider what I'm about to say when we see the doctor.

"Mrs. Simpson," a loud voice calls out. The nurse waves for us to come through the doorway. Mom struggles to get out of the chair, rises up a few inches, then flops back into it. She tries again, this time pressing on the handle of her oxygen cart, but her legs give out before she can stand. I offer her my hand but she refuses. On her third try, she propels herself out of the chair and speeds towards the door. As we follow, the woman says, "Dr. Sanders was called out on an emergency, and Morgan, our physician's assistant, will see you."

I'm not happy with this unforeseen change, but focus my energy on the words I have to say for my mother. Her life rests in my hands, and my hands are slick with doubt about my ability to give her the best care. We'll both drown if I have to paddle alone while she holds on to me. I can't let her down, and I know that I won't.

Once we're in the exam room, Mom struggles to climb onto the narrow table, refusing my offer to help. After she manages to settle herself on the paper-lined table, the nurse places a thermometer in Mom's mouth and takes her blood pressure. She writes in Mom's chart, tells us Morgan will be in to see us in a few minutes, and leaves.

I take those minutes alone to remind Mom that I'm going to ask Morgan to get her into hospice. I want to make certain Mom hasn't stuffed our conversation down that mysterious place inside herself where unpleasant things disappear and are never heard of again. I'd like her to be as comfortable as possible given the situation we're in, but can a person in quicksand ever relax?

The door opens and in swoops a petite, serious-looking woman in a doctor's white coat. She goes over to my mother and in a distracted manner says, "Mrs. Simpson, I'm Morgan."

"Hello, Morgan," Mom says with an inviting smile. She's on good behavior.

"I'm Dr. Sanders' physician's assistant." She swivels my way and glances down at Mom's chart, and although she looks up, never makes eye contact. "And you must be her daughter, Virginia."

After I acknowledge that I am, she says, "Are you okay with my examining your mother in place of Dr. Sanders?"

I hesitate because I'm not sure whether her presence will put a kink in my plans. I decide we need to take care of this today and ask Mom if she's okay with it. After she agrees, Morgan starts to examine her.

I consider what I'm going to say when she finishes. As she stands at the counter writing on Mom's chart, I say, "Morgan, I'd like to talk to you about something."

"Oh," she says as she looks at me over her shoulder.

"I'd like to get my mom into hospice."

Without any hesitation, she spins to face me, and with the compassion of a district attorney, says, "Oh, do you think your mother has only six months to live?"

What an idiot! I'd like to see to it she has only six seconds to live. I imagine myself leaping across the room, grasping her neck with both hands, and shaking her. She has no idea of my nefarious thoughts as I wear my best poker face. I glance over at Mom, who pretends to study her hands.

My jaw clenches so tight I'm surprised I can speak, but manage to hiss, "E-yes, I do," with a curt nod. I peek at Mom. She doesn't look at me, and I wish she hadn't heard any of this, but I know she has. There's nothing wrong with Mom's hearing, although deafness would be a gift right now.

"You understand this means that her care will be palliative and no measures will be taken to prolong her life," Morgan-the-obtuse says.

"Yes, I understand." I'm rigid with anger but try to look composed.

Morgan shifts her attention to Mom. "Do you understand everything we've talked about, Mrs. Simpson, and do you agree?"

"Yes," Mom says but keeps her eyes on her hands.

"Okay, I'll write out the prescription. Do you have a hospice in mind?"

"Yes, I do," I say, and give her the name of Carol's hospice.

———

Once Mom and I are in the car and on our way home, I begin damage control. My hands clutch the steering wheel. "Mom, I don't think you only have six months to live, but I had to say I did so that we could get you better care like we discussed Tuesday."

"You said what you needed to say." Her voice is mild.

"Are you okay?" I glance at her.

"Yes, Ginni." She doesn't look my way.

Mom is silent the rest of the ride home. I honor her silence by remaining quiet, staying in my own spiraling thoughts.

Chapter 21:

Hospice

*You matter because you are you, and you matter to the
end of your life. We will do all we can not only to help
you die peacefully, but also to live until you die.*

—Dame Cicely Saunders, founder of
the hospice movement

WEDNESDAY, NOVEMBER 17, 2004

Despite the bright sun and comfortable 79 degrees, I shiver as I
drive home for Mom's appointment with the hospice team. In
November the desert is reborn like a dormant flower blossom-
ing anew. The difference is our desert blooms with people we
call "Snowbirds" because they flee colder states to enjoy our mild
winter and spring. The streets, so barren between May and Oc-

tober, fill with cars. El Paseo beckons these wealthy patrons, who spend enough money to keep shops and restaurants alive during the empty, hot summer. The vibrancy and aliveness all around me are the antithesis of my current life.

Today, strangers from hospice will invade our home and become the people Mom and I rely on. This will not be easy for two independent women like us.

Mom is in the family room watching TV with Sunny and Sophie at her side. Both girls get up when I enter, offer those special tail-wag hellos, and I can't help but smile, even on a day that feels solemn as a funeral.

I join Mom on the couch but soon the doorbell chimes its feeble, one-note ding, a sound so quiet I almost miss it. I spring off the couch and head to the door. I find two women, one in a shapeless business suit and the younger one in a blue blouse and floral, ankle-length skirt that harkens back to the hippie days of the 1970s.

"We're with hospice and we're here to see Ruth Simpson," the woman in the gray suit says.

"You've got the right house," I smile. "I'm her daughter, Virginia." I welcome them in.

"Mom," I call out, "the ladies from hospice are here."

"I know," she says as she rises from her spot on the couch. She comes toward the door, but pauses and waits for the hospice ladies to approach her. Some might think she's aloof, but I know better: my mother is shy and lacks the warm social skills that would invite others to enter her world. The ladies are not put off by her manner and greet her with broad smiles.

"Let's sit here," I say as I step towards the living room. Mom descends onto the creamy chenille couch and the ladies perch next to her, one on each side.

"Ruth, I'm Helen, the administrative officer with hospice," says the suit lady, a woman in her late sixties. She wears her dusty brown hair short with tight curls. Severe lines etched on her face are a contrast to her robust warm voice. She gestures to the floral lady, whose hair cascades in loose curls past her shoulders. "This is Sandra, the social worker assigned to you. Janet, who will be your head nurse, should be here in a few minutes."

I assume Sandra is near my age because of the fine lines around her eyes.

Mom massages her bony hands like she's rubbing cream into them and remains silent throughout the introductions. Her body is stiff and her face neutral. I start to sit down when the doorbell rings. I open the door to Janet, a robust woman who appears to be in her late forties. Her long, unruly blonde hair flows to the center of her ample chest. She wears khaki pants, clogs, and a blue scrub top. Janet greets me with an open, no-agenda smile and introduces herself. We shake hands, and I tell her to call me Ginni. As we enter, Janet calls out hellos to Helen and Sandra, then introduces herself to Mom. Mom returns the greeting with a flat smile, meek hello, and a quick, dainty handshake.

I invite Janet to sit. She drops her black bag to the floor and joins the gathering.

I scan this group of women who look like they could be four ladies gathered for an afternoon tea, then remember my manners and ask, "Can I offer you ladies anything to drink—juice, water? I'm sorry I don't have any soda."

"No, thank you," Helen says. "We're fine."

"I'd like some cranberry raspberry juice," Mom says in a voice sweeter and higher than normal.

"One cranberry raspberry juice coming up." I rush to the kitchen. I'm gone less than a minute, but by the time I return, they're already engrossed in conversation and I almost feel like an intruder when I hand Mom her juice. I plop into my chair, cross my legs, and, like an observer across a faraway chasm, I watch.

Mom holds herself still and straight as a starched shirt, which is in contrast to the drape of her shapeless black-and-white balloon of a blouse. I think of it as her uniform, because she wears it most days. Mom used to wear classic tailored blouses with crisp collars, and this loose blouse doesn't fit the image I still carry of my stylish mother.

Helen pulls out a stack of papers from her briefcase and offers a brochure to Mom. "Ruth, this will tell you about our organization."

Mom drops it on her lap without a glance. She sips her juice, puts the glass down on the coffee table, and rubs her hands.

Helen continues. "I need to go over the rest of these papers with you and then have you sign them. They will give us permission to care for you and let us order your current prescriptions and any other medications we deem necessary to keep you comfortable. Dr. Hyde, our hospice physician, will visit you within a week."

I've become accustomed to people discussing Mom with me even when she's there, but today, these ladies offer Mom the full respect any adult about to make one of the biggest commitments in her life deserves. I'm impressed and relieved. Their actions take the pressure off me to choose what my mother may or may not want as her health declines.

I try to focus on what Helen is saying, but my thoughts scatter like random jigsaw pieces. If I have any emotions about what's going on, I can't find them. I'm just a body in the room hearing sounds that never reach inside. I know this doesn't mean I'm not feeling anything. It's more likely that a flood of emotions is at a crescendo, and I'm overwhelmed to the point of being numb. My focus is on Mom, and it isn't until she speaks that I can hear what's being said.

Helen pauses and, with a pen in hand, asks Mom if she has any questions.

"I need to read these documents before I sign them," Mom says, and glances over at me. "Right, Ginni?"

"Right, Mom." I nod.

After Mom looks over the papers, she asks Helen for her pen, and just as she's about to sign, she tilts her head, pulls the pen off the paper, and says, "Helen?"

"Yes, Ruth."

"What happens if I change my mind? What if I decide I don't want hospice?" Mom surprises me with her calm assurance at a time I assume would be very emotional for most people. She's her old, professional self.

Helen looks straight into Mom's eyes and in a tender voice says, "Ruth, you have the right at any time to stop hospice care and return to your medical doctor. This is all your choice, and you should be comfortable with your decision. I want you to know that even if you decide to stop, you can always choose to start with us again. We're here to make your life easier, and one way we do this is by making certain you have a say over your own life." While Helen speaks, Mom never takes her eyes off her, and she nods in acknowledgement.

I like Helen's answer, because it's in alignment with my belief that we each have only one death, and the person dying should be the one to decide how she's going to do it.

"I need to go over your mother's medication with you," I hear Janet say as if through a distant cloud.

"What?"

"Let's you and I go into the kitchen, where we can discuss your mother's medications."

"Now?" I squint at her.

"Sure. They don't need us to be here right now." She tilts her head towards the trio on the couch.

"Okay."

Once we're in the kitchen, Janet tells me they will write a prescription for Advair and Albuterol to help Mom with her breathing. I feel sick when she adds, "We're including liquid morphine. Be sure and keep it in the refrigerator. You'll need it near the end of your mother's life to manage her pain."

Of all the things going on, this is what gets me, what terrifies me. *I can't administer morphine to my mother. I'm not a doctor. I don't know how. What if I give her too little? What if I give her too much? What if I kill her?*

My thoughts are stopped on their racetrack when Sandra enters with a DNR, Do Not Resuscitate Order, signed by Mom. As she tapes it to the front of the refrigerator, she turns her attention to me. "Be sure and keep this on the refrigerator so our team knows your mother's wishes. If something happens to your mother when we're not here, call us and not the fire department or police, because if you call them, the paramedics will perform CPR even if she's already dead. They have to, and this isn't anything you want to see."

I envision myself hysterical and screaming as I watch large men pound on my dead mother's tiny, lifeless body and crush her fragile bones into powder. I shake my head to reset the picture. I sigh and steady myself to be able to take all this in.

I guess the hospice team has finished, because Helen gathers up the papers on the coffee table, sorts them into two piles, and offers a stack to Mom. "These are for you, Ruth. Keep them in a safe place."

"Give them to Ginni," Mom says. Helen stretches across the coffee table and I grab the papers.

Helen turns her attention back to Mom, takes her hand, and says, "Ruth, it was our pleasure to meet you. I promise we'll take good care of you."

"I hope so," Mom says, her voice low and somber.

I walk the ladies to the door and thank them for coming. I close the door and turn back towards Mom. She's headed toward her room.

I catch up with her and say, "Mom, are you okay? Would you like to talk?"

She shakes her head. "I'm fine, Ginni. I just want to go to my room and lie down for a while."

"Okay, Mom." I'm about to reach out to hug her, but her blue eyes, small and dark with a familiar determination, are a stop sign. This is a time to let her be. She's not me. I'd be a puddle, and a hug would be the only thing to give me strength. I respect her way. I didn't always, but her stoicism and pragmatic resolve in action have renewed my admiration for her.

My love continues to grow along with my sorrow.

I sigh a lot these days. I sigh, and hot tears are ready to push up from my chest and tumble down my cheeks. I don't allow them. Now is not the time. I'll cry when Mom is in her room watching TV. I'll cry behind my closed door on the other side of the house. I'll get in the shower and cry. Cry for Mom, and cry for me. I hope the tears won't make my eyes red and puffy and that Mom won't notice.

I again resolve to comfort and care for her as she did for me so many years when I was often a sick little girl who trapped her in the house because I was home from school. I want to give back to Mom now and nurture her as she did me. I want to make whatever is left of her life as comfortable as possible. I want her to know she is loved.

I've accomplished everything I set out to do these past few weeks, but there's no pleasure in getting what I want. The only victory would be for my mom to be healthy, vibrant, and not dying. I know this wish is futile, but I still want the one thing I cannot have. As the days and months march on, I know I'll be confronted at ever-increasing levels with how little control we humans have and how traumatic it is to watch someone we love fade away in bits and pieces while we are helpless bystanders. Bob understands this only too well, and I'm fortunate he entered my life when he did. He can't fix anything, but knowing he's a phone call away and visits every ten to fourteen days bolsters my strength to deal with the day-to-day challenges confronting Mom and me.

Chapter 22:

Last Thanksgiving

Every day should be passed as if it were to be our last.
—Publilius Syrus

NOVEMBER 25, 2004

Thanksgiving is the only holiday Mom and I always celebrate together, and I sense this will be our last. I know this in my body and only allow a faint whisper of it in my thoughts.

Bob won't be with us because he spends Thanksgivings in Ohio with his deceased wife Flo's parents, Bill and Pearl. When Flo died her parents were left childless, having lost Flo's older brother in a plane accident years before her death. Bob promised Flo he would look after her parents and he continues to honor his promise. In October, Bill died, and I told Bob to invite Pearl to come to the desert so she wouldn't be alone. Pearl appreciated the invitation but declined because of hip surgery and her advanced age. Bob is the kind of person who would never abandon Pearl. As much as I would like him to be with Mom and me, I respect and love him for his loyalty.

I am determined to create a delicious dinner for Mom, and to pay attention to these precious moments with my mother that will never come again. I feel lucky—not lucky that Mom is dying, but I'm fortunate I can do something special for her to celebrate Thanksgiving.

I cast aside my sadness and put on my happy face to convince myself I still feel the joy of cooking Thanksgiving dinner that I've always had. I'm no culinary diva. I could be the wife Rodney Dangerfield referred to when he said he took his wife somewhere she'd never been before—the kitchen. But I've prepared this meal for us many times over the years, and I move around the kitchen with confidence. The pungent aroma of white wine, onions, carrots, celery, garlic, and chopped turkey giblets and neck boiling on the stove will be transmuted into a luscious brown gravy when turkey drippings, Madeira, Kitchen Bouquet, and flour are added. If only there were ingredients I could add to my twig-thin mother to transform her into the robust woman she once was.

Mom watches me from her perch on one of the two bar stools at the kitchen counter as we reminisce about past Thanksgivings.

"I remember when I was seven and you didn't realize you were sick until someone found ground glass in the Jell-O mold," I say as I stir more sage into the stuffing. Mom always claimed to be as befuddled about how that day unfolded as the rest of us.

"I had pneumonia."

"I know. It was the only time you were ever sick. It seemed like you were in bed forever. I missed you the most the night Dad cooked dinner. He scrambled eggs and let me sit in his seat on the orange banquette in the kitchen. I took a bite, scrunched my nose and mouth, and whined, 'These taste terrible.'

"'No they don't,' Dad roared like an angry lion. 'Eat them!'

"They were so bad, Mom, and I had no choice but to sit there and choke down each bite while Dad watched to make sure I finished."

Through giggles, Mom says, "Ginni, I'll tell you something."

"What, Mom?" I ask, my eyes wide with amusement. I'm fascinated to hear what she'll say, because my mother doesn't giggle.

"Your father came into the bedroom, all sheepish, and admitted he'd poured eggnog instead of milk into the eggs."

"Tsk," I shake my head. "Typical that he wouldn't admit to his kids he'd made a mistake. You're just lucky you didn't eat them. They were God-awful. Yick." I stick out my tongue.

Mom pulls a piece of Kleenex from her sleeve and wipes her moist eyes as she full-out laughs. Her joy is contagious.

I spoon cornbread stuffing into the turkey and the rest into a casserole. I glance over at the sink and remember Mom and I collaborating on her apple pie filling.

"Gee, I miss your apple pie, Mom. Yours was the best."

"I couldn't have done it without your nose."

———

Mom always called me over to sniff test her apple pie mixture to make sure she had the right ratio of sugar, cinnamon, and lemon zest stirred over the pippin apple slices. I bet she didn't need me but wanted me to feel part of creating her dessert since I hadn't learned to make pies. She tried to teach me, but when I couldn't get the wrist action to mix the crust, she took over and never offered any more pie crust lessons.

She also gave up on teaching me when she tried to give me a crash course on football when I was eighteen. A tall, tan fraternity boy from the University of Southern California asked me to the annual USC-UCLA football game, and of course I said an enthusiastic yes and didn't mention I'd never seen a football game.

"Mom, mom, I need your help," I called out as soon as I got off the phone.

Ten minutes is all it took for her to realize I didn't understand any of her explanations. She huffed and said, "Ginni, when everyone around you cheers and looks happy, you cheer and look happy. And when they look unhappy, you look unhappy."

Her instructions worked. My date had no clue I didn't follow even one second of the game that day.

⁓

Today, I try to act upbeat for Mom's sake as I bustle around the kitchen, but this Thanksgiving brings a similar kind of "joy" as the Thanksgiving in 1961, three days after my dad died. On that Thanksgiving, death had already invaded our family, and on this one, death lies ahead of us. I have no idea how I will manage a Thanksgiving without my mother. She is Thanksgiving to me and has been since Dad died. He took with him so many things, but the one tradition we have always kept is Thanksgiving.

I don't recall any Thanksgivings celebrated with my father. I was young and didn't pay much attention to his presence, yet his absence continues to loom over my life whether I think about him or not.

After Dad died, I grew fearful of my own death and afraid my mother would die. I carried the burden of those fears with me far too many years. When I was in my twenties, my therapist said I had a "phobic fear of death." I decided to face my fear, and began to read everything I could find on death and dying. I went to the downtown Los Angeles Library, and the one book I found declared that children who'd lost a parent in childhood were often doomed to kill themselves when they became adults. I slammed it closed and whispered in exasperation to myself, "Well, that wasn't very useful." Bookstores carried few, if any, books on death, and when they did, for some inexplicable reason, they were always next to the section on sex. I've always wondered why but guessed that talking about sex and death was taboo.

I have been afraid of Mom dying since I was twelve, but anticipating with certainty that Mom will die soon is different. When I was a teenager, I thought my middle age and Mom's old age were at the end of a long tunnel, far away. I couldn't know until I got where I am now that the end seems to come quicker than a blink, and as near as the next breath. Death close up, a total annihilation and the person forever gone, is more unfathomable than death in the distant future. I march through the days less fearful than when I was young, yet every ounce of me is filled with the essence of doom. I balance between reality and wishful thinking.

Decades ago I chose to study death as a way of coping with my fears. Yet despite everything I've learned through my education and years as a professional helping grieving people and companioning those who are dying, I am surprised to find myself filled with the same confusion, denials, and moments of emotional unbalance as any layperson.

What will happen when my mother dies? We like to joke

that she will visit me. I've asked her to promise she'll never show up in my bedroom when Bob and I are making love. She offered an impish smile. "I think that would be fun."

"Well I don't, Mom, so promise me," I said with a laugh.

"Oh, okay," she grinned.

I won't find out until she dies whether she will visit. Her death might mean that I'll never see or hear from her again. When Dad died, he disappeared with no warning, and our relationship has only existed in the conversations I have with him in my head. Maybe it will be different with Mom—we've had years to forge a strong connection based not only on being mother and daughter, but on a friendship that has outlasted disagreements, arguments, and irritations.

All the books and studies I've read on anticipatory grief seem wrong to me. I do not grieve in anticipation of my mother's death. I grieve for the aspects of my mother that I lose each day as her health declines. I miss her youth, her vibrance, independence, competence, and the ways she was always interested in me and my life.

Yet as long as she continues to breathe, I will view our time as a gift to heal the tears that have worn into the fabric of our relationship, and I will find the joy in what we have today.

Mom stands near me as I open the oven and take out the now browned turkey. Smiling, she says it looks delicious and she can't wait to taste it. Her words are more nourishing to me than the food I will eat tonight.

The doorbell rings, but before I can answer it, Sunny and George, a couple in their seventies, enter with big smiles and outstretched arms. Sunny, a portly woman with short white hair, has become a confidant and one of my dearest friends. She likes to think I named my dog Sunny after her, and I let her believe it's true. George, a skinny man with a shock of thick white hair and a devilish yet kind gleam in his eyes, is never without a joke. He likes to refer to himself as "Bond, James Bond." They each hug me, then turn their attention to my mother.

"Ruth, you look gorgeous," Sunny says as she throws her arms around Mom. George stands next to them with a big smile on his handsome face, and as soon as Sunny releases Mom, he steps in for a hug. The doorbell rings again and my friends Cindy and her partner Theresa enter, offering an apple pie to join the pumpkin cheesecake I've made. Cindy has known Mom and me for the past five years and is close to both of us. Her simple smile belies a fierce intelligence. Theresa is shorter than Cindy and has dark hair and skin in contrast to Cindy's freckled, fair complexion and wheat-blonde hair. After they hug and kiss Mom, Cindy and Theresa talk with Sunny and George like they're old friends.

While everyone mingles in the living room, I take the orange praline yams and stuffing out of the oven before turning the turkey drippings into a delicious gravy. Mom joins me and settles herself on the bar stool across from me at the stove. I add Madeira to the drippings. When I open the bag of flour, Mom says, "Now remember to put the liquid into the flour and mix them together before you pour it into the gravy." Knowing she needs to feel useful, I say nothing about the many times I've done this over the years. Instead, I thank her for making sure I do it right.

When the gravy is ready, I ask George to carve the turkey. Mom never takes her eyes off him as he slices. Mom has always prided herself on her carving ability, so I'm sure it takes all of her willpower to let him do it his way and not correct him.

When we're all seated at the table, I thank everyone for joining Mom and me on our favorite holiday. I focus my attention on Mom and say, "I love you very much and hope you and all our guests enjoy the meal." I don't tell anyone that my smile hides the ache I feel knowing this will be the last time Mom and I will celebrate Thanksgiving. Tonight is for good times and creating good memories.

And as has become so true of late, after we've eaten our Thanksgiving meal, and the guests have gone home and Mom is asleep, I go to my room and cry. Watching her unrelenting move towards death is harder than my worst childhood nightmares.

Chapter 23:

Not So Merry Christmas

*My idea of Christmas, whether old-fashioned or modern,
is very simple: loving others. Come to think of it, why do
we have to wait for Christmas to do that?*

—Bob Hope

DECEMBER 23–25, 2004

In two days we'll celebrate Christmas. It will be like a show that
opens and closes on the same night, because it's the first time
Mom and I have celebrated together since Dad died and the last
one that she and I will share. Since his death, Christmas for our
family has always meant no gifts, no gathering, and no meal—
just another day on its way to the end of the year. Since she's lived
with me, Mom's always gone to Los Angeles to play bridge with

her girlfriends and celebrate the holiday with Peter and Ellyn.

She is no longer well enough to travel, so I plan to celebrate with an extra-special meal full of foods I'll prepare for the first time: prime rib with whipped horseradish, Yorkshire pudding, Gulliver's creamed spinach, and a hot fruit casserole. The taste of prime rib will take us both back to those special occasions when I was a child and we would go to Lawry's Prime Rib on La Cienega Boulevard in Los Angeles. Dessert will be Mom's cheesecake.

For years when I'd ask for the recipe, she'd reply, "I can always make one for you."

I wanted that recipe, so about fifteen years ago, after she'd refused yet again, I said, "I can just see myself leaning over your coffin saying, 'But Mom, you forgot to give me the recipe!'"

"Tsk. All right, all right, I'll give it to you."

Perhaps my method was somewhat underhanded, and maybe you could call it a bit of skullduggery, but she gave me her recipe written on an index card. For the rest of my life, whenever I need a bit of my childhood and my mother, I will prepare her cheesecake.

This Christmas, I want our house to feel warm with great food, friends, and laughter. I'll do anything to hide our reality, if only for a few hours. I hope to create a memory that Mom and I can cherish. I have so few special holiday memories that connect the threads of my life that now I race against time to generate something I can hold on to next year and all the years that follow.

⌣

The first Christmas I can remember was when I was four years old. As soon as I woke up my head sprang off the pillow and my body yanked upright, ready to race to the living room to see what Santa left for me under the tree, but I couldn't open my eyes. They were stuck together like they'd been glued shut. I lifted my eyebrows, struggled with every muscle in my face, and tried to open them with my fingers, but the lids wouldn't part. I was afraid if I didn't get to the tree soon, my presents and Christmas would be gone. I never found out why my eyes got stuck together. That moment melted away, and then I was six years old walking to school singing "White Choral Bells" with my best friend, Alene.

What I remember most about Christmas before Dad died were the presents Mom had hidden behind the pink chaise in her bedroom. I'd skulk across the teeny hallway between our rooms and slip the ribbon off each package, carefully lifting the edge of the tissue so I could peek at my gift—most of the time it was clothes from high-end department stores like Bullocks Wilshire, I. Magnin, or Robinson's in Beverly Hills. Mom shopped as if we had a lot of money, so I thought we were rich. When I was nine, for reasons I'll never understand, my parents gave me a black Mattel machine gun, which bore little resemblance to the automated toy guns of today. When I turned the crank it would rat-a-tat-a-tat as I ran around shooting at my friends, who'd shoot back with cap guns that made a loud pop and emitted a puff of smoke.

Now I'm fifty-five and I don't want to close my eyes this Christmas and find Mom is gone and slipped into my past like that Christmas long ago. I'm so glad Bob's here for Christmas. We had to scrap plans for me to go to Texas, like I did last year, to celebrate with him. His home is the only place I can sleep, because there I am free of responsibility.

Bob is my oasis. He's more familiar with the pain of watching a loved one die than most people—his first son not even two when he died, his best childhood friend dead at thirty-nine, his wife, Flo, gone at fifty-five, and this year his best friend, Mike, who was sixty-one, and Bob's father-in-law in October. When he isn't here, Bob calls every day. Though his calls have meant a lot since the moment we met, they are now my lifeline. He makes me laugh and listens without trying to fix me. He says he holds me in his heart and prayers. And he tells me he loves me.

Without Bob, I'd be more alone than I feel as I wait for a future I dread. Few of my friends remember to call and check on us. I think because the person dying is old and is my mother, our situation doesn't seem like much of an event to them—at least not an event worthy of a card or a weekly phone call just to say, "Hi. I'm thinking of you." I can't fault them. They've never been through this and have no clue about the isolation and pain of being a caretaker and watching someone you love die.

Mom's only visitors are the incredible hospice nurses who come by once or twice a week and spend at least a half hour chatting while they check her vital signs. They have become angels and blessings to us both. They arrive with hugs, and one nurse brought Mom chocolates, my mother's favorite. Mom's friends, the same ones who gossiped that *I* was a bad daughter, never call and never visit.

⁓

I found out about Mom's friends' nasty chatter last month while I networked for my Center at a Palm Desert Chamber Mixer held at the Joselyn Senior Center.

I was in a circle laughing with some friends when Michael, the handsome executive director of the senior center, strode over to join us. He had a scowl on his face, and his first words were, "I've heard you abandoned your mother."

Ambushed, my stomach contracted in a spasm as if I'd been

kicked in the gut and I folded my arms across my chest. I took a deep breath before I spoke, because my energy was hot, and I didn't want to sound angry.

"What are you talking about? My mother lives with me and I see her every day."

"I'm so relieved." The coldness was gone from his voice and he smiled.

Too little too late for me. I was fuming that people had said this to him and that Michael believed them.

"Good. I'm glad that's cleared up for you. You'll have to excuse me," I said, and headed to the door to go home.

As soon as I got there, I marched into Mom's room and told her what Michael had said to me. I had no idea where he got his information. I didn't think that Mom had said anything, because as far as I knew, she hadn't talked to her senior center friends in a long time. I wanted to share with her what I'd heard.

"Oh, some people can't take a joke," she said, making a face and looking uncomfortable.

I peered over the top of my glasses. "Mom, even joking you can't tell people I've abandoned you. You have to be careful what you say and can't kid about things like this because if someone takes you seriously, they could claim senior abuse and remove you from my care."

Her eyes were big, her brow furrowed. "Okay, Ginni. I won't say anything to anyone again."

I am furious that negative busybodies who do nothing for Mom have the gall to judge and complain about me. I am the one who calls all the time, even when I've just left the house to do some errands. I am the one in the trenches day in and day out. How dare they criticize me when they know nothing about our daily life?

As the weeks passed, there was more to worry about than gossip. Today, as she is leaving, I escort Janice to the front door. She stops before we get there and turns towards me.

"Ginni, one of your mom's lungs has completely stopped working and the other sounds raspy."

"What does this mean? How long will she live?"

"With congestive heart failure, sometimes patients do fine for quite a while and then go into a sudden decline and die." In what seems like a non sequitur, she adds, "You need to spend more time with your mother."

I feel defeated. I don't know what more I can do. Do they want me to cut a vein and bleed to keep Mom happy? Drained and exhausted, I don't know how to respond.

Janice mistakes what could be a look of alarm on my face, and touches my arm. "Don't worry. Your mother's going to live a long time."

But I won't. I'm not young anymore, and feel wearier than I've ever been. I wonder how much stress my body can tolerate before it gives out.

"Thanks for coming, Janice." I take her arm and lead her to the front door. I'm glad the hospice people visit so Mom gets to see people besides me, but I need Janice to go so I can be alone and sort out my feelings.

In the last few months, Mom has had other visitors besides the hospice team, but all of them are dead. The first to come were her husbands, Jimmy and my dad. Next was my mother's mother, who came to see how she was. My mother, a woman who never cries, cried when she told me she saw her mother. Her most recent visitor was a little girl.

"A little girl, five or six years old, came today. She looked like you but she wasn't you."

"Do you think she was your first daughter, the one who died when you were six months pregnant?"

"Yes. I think it was her."

The only who hasn't shown up is my grandfather. I think he'll be the last one and then she'll be ready to go.

Her visitors astonish Mom. "After all, I don't believe in these kinds of things. Can you believe this is happening to me?"

"Yes, Mom. I believe they are real."

"Me, too."

Because Mom has always been an atheist and not spiritual, I am comforted by her visitors. In a book I read entitled *Final Gifts*, by Maggie Callanan and Patricia Kelley, I learned these visits are called Nearing Death Awareness. Nearing Death Awareness occurs across all cultures and religions and is a common experience of people at the end of their lives. People who died before them, even when the one dying doesn't know that the person visiting has already passed away, often visit terminally ill people.

I am relieved to know Mom will not be alone when she dies, and excited for her that she will get to be with people who love her enough to come back to help her on this new journey.

I have no idea when Mom will leave, so all I can do is live today. Bob has arrived from Texas, and I've invited other people my mother likes to join us—Sunny and George, who were with us for Thanksgiving, and Julie, a short blonde woman who is a psychologist and my closest girlfriend in the desert.

My mother is in everything I do today. My love for her is in all the details, from the food I've chosen to the guests, and even the table I set with my best china and three crystal candleholders Mom gave me many years ago.

She watches from her perch on the bar chair at the kitchen island as I prepare the prime rib and Yorkshire pudding, unaware that the main ingredient I am adding is my love for her. I observe her even as I focus on the food. If she knows this is her last Christmas or the reasons I'm preparing this special evening for her, she never says, and I don't tell her. I follow her lead: she doesn't share what she may be feeling about this being the last Christmas or her appreciation of everything I'm doing, so I stay silent.

Around two o'clock, Mom announces she's going to take a nap. Sunny and Sophie follow her, tails wagging. While Mom sleeps, I prepare the rest of the food with as much care as if I were hosting royalty. Tonight is special. Every holiday, every dinner, every moment should be special, but the knowledge that this is our final Christmas adds to this day of preparation.

A few hours later, Bob and I are dressed and in the kitchen when Mom enters looking pretty in a turquoise cable-knit sweater. Bob rises from his chair, kisses her cheek, and tells her how pretty she looks. He's about to pour her a glass of wine when the doorbell rings. Bob goes to the front door and Mom stands up to greet Sunny and George, who head towards Mom with their arms open, ready to envelope her with hugs.

"Ruth, you look beautiful," Sunny says. Even though she smiles, Mom shakes her head as if to say, *No, I don't.*

Once Julie arrives, I lay out a platter of cheeses, and everyone visits in the living room while I return to the kitchen to finish the gravy.

I am relieved that the roast has morphed into a beautiful prime rib. While Bob carves the roast and places it on a large, white, oval platter surrounded by the individual Yorkshire puddings, I put the rest of the food into serving pieces and call everyone to the table.

I sit at the head of the table, with Mom to my left, and wait to see if she enjoys the food. She smiles as she takes her first bites and I breathe a sigh of relief. Watching her eat with a relish I haven't seen in more than a year makes me feel as though my whole body is smiling.

I feel good that I have accomplished what I set out to do. I've created a Christmas to make up for all the lost Christmases and all the rest that will never be.

Chapter 24:

Wake Up!

If you're going through hell, keep going.
—*Winston Churchill*

DECEMBER 29, 2004

I'm asleep, and in my dream a high-pitched buzz screeches from inside a gloomy dusk.

Then I'm awake and hear a shrill ambulance siren streak by. No, it's not an ambulance; it must be my tinnitus. The room is dark except for shadows sifting through the shutter slats. I sit up and turn my head to listen, hearing nothing but middle-of-the-night silence. I turn the other way and the buzz returns. Sunny and Sophie are stretched across the end of the bed. Both gaze at me for a moment, then grunt as they lower their heads down.

They would react if they heard the noise, so I decide the source of the thrum is from inside my head.

I lie down, ready to fall back to sleep, when, like a sharp slap across the face, I realize what the loud buzz means and shoot out of bed. *The compressor! Something is wrong with Mom's oxygen supply.* I zoom towards her room, tailed by Sunny and Sophie close at my heels. I stop at her bathroom. The compressor blares at an ear-shattering level and the gauge reads, "Oxygen low."

I dash into her room to see if she's still alive. She's awake and upright, resting against the headboard. Sophie lies at Mom's feet and Sunny sits on the floor with her nose on the bed. I stop to catch my breath before I speak.

"Mom, how are you?" I examine her to determine how she's doing.

"Fine," she says with a cursory glance my direction. Her voice is calm and her face as serene as a meditating yogi. She acts like my checking on her at four thirty in the morning is nothing out of the ordinary.

Back in the bathroom, I fiddle with the machine until everything reads normal, the buzz stops, and the familiar, rhythmic *pop, swoosh* resumes. I return to Mom and check the cannula to make sure the line is clear.

"Easier to breathe?"

"Yes."

"Good. I'm going back to bed."

"All right, Ginni," she says in a sweet whisper.

"Sunny, Sophie, want to come with me?" They don't move. They roll their eyes, their eyebrows wiggle, and they look around as though they've decided to pretend they no longer understand anything I say. "Okay, okay, I get it. Stay with her, you traitors."

Mom laughs.

I'm glad they've decided to watch over her. I pad back to my room and climb into my empty bed. I flail back and forth for the next half hour, alert to every sound, too tense to sleep. My mind is abuzz with nervous, unintelligible chatter and the ever-present tinnitus chime. I give up on sleep, get out of bed, and head for the kitchen to make a pot of coffee. As I pour the grounds into the paper filter, Sunny and Sophie join me with tail-wagging hellos. I smile and reach down to pet them. They don't tell me their secrets, but I sometimes wonder if they're wiser than we are because they understand the importance of celebrating each moment. I let the girls outside while the coffee perks. When they return, I give them their favorite peanut butter treats, and they head back to Mom's room, biscuits in their mouths.

At six o'clock, I walk outside in the dark to retrieve the morning paper. I'm anxious to read the latest news about the disaster that occurred three days ago off the west coast of Sumatra. An earthquake estimated at a magnitude between 9.1 and 9.3 was followed by a tsunami that killed thousands of people in fourteen countries. The death toll continues to rise.

The paper isn't there. The carrier must be late due to last night's rain. Half an hour later, when the paper still hasn't arrived, I call to find out what happened. The woman on the other end of the phone says, "Our carrier quit his route halfway through. It happens quite often." She relates this as if that makes it okay that there is no paper. When I ask if someone else will deliver the paper she says that's not likely. I'm annoyed but I don't have the energy to argue through the impasse we've reached.

When dawn breaks across the darkness, I check on Mom. She's awake and hasn't moved from where I left her.

"How're you feeling, Mom?"

"Not so good." Her right hand is on her chest. Her normally flushed skin is a pale gray.

I sit next to her. "I'm sorry, Mom. Did you hear the alarm a few hours ago?"

"Yes, but I didn't know what to do about it and didn't want to bother you."

I take her hand. It's ice-cube cold, and I need to rub it to increase her circulation. "It's important you do something or call me when you hear anything that isn't normal or you're having trouble breathing." My voice is higher than normal. I'm scared, and fear grabs my throat. "Call for me any time. That's why I gave you the pager when you moved in—so that you could contact me across the house without having to get out of bed or yell. Okay?" I wait for her to respond.

Silence.

"Okay?" My neck juts forward and I peer at her over my glasses.

"Fine." Her voice is flat.

Mom's breathing changes. Her chest rises and falls in intermittent, sudden, jerky movements.

"Trouble breathing?"

She nods yes.

"I'll be right back." I race to the kitchen, gather her breathing medicines—Albuterol and Advair—and hurry back to her room.

I hold the nebulizer to Mom's mouth, and once she has her lips around it, I press down to deliver the Albuterol, a bronchodilator that relaxes and opens the air passages to her lungs. Next comes the Advair, a purple disk, which reduces irritation and swelling of her airways. Her eyes always widen when she inhales the Advair. I relax as the color begins to return to her face.

It's kind of ironic that I care for Mom's lungs since once upon a time she took care of mine. I contracted a severe case of bronchitis when I was seven and honked my way through the next two years, especially when the weather changed. Mom gave me pills every morning and afternoon, and now I give her many pills every day. She made sure my hydrocollator filled with stinky medicine was plugged in wherever I was so it could spew the steam to clear my lungs. Now I watch after her lungs. In the 1950s, no one realized the connection between smoking and the illnesses I had then and Mom has now. Both Mom and Dad smoked cigarettes, and the inside of our house was always filled with a toxic gray cloud. I suppose this played a part in my dad's early death, and I'm certain the years of cigarettes are killing Mom now.

Mom and I both stopped smoking long ago, and we now live in a smoke-free home. Mom smoked more than fifty years. She was a healthy seventy-five when she smoked her last cigarette, but she was too late to prevent the diseases that appeared more than a decade later and now suck away her life. Because I smoked for a much shorter time and quit six years before she did, I hope it was soon enough so I won't experience what she is going through.

———

I've showered and dressed by the time Bob arrives from Dallas at ten. After he kisses me and says hello to Mom, he changes into shorts and a T-shirt and goes for a run. While he's out, I unload the dishwasher from last night, and as I ruminate over the events of this morning, I am gobsmacked by the realization Mom would have let herself die if the alarm hadn't been loud enough to awaken me. Sadness floods my body. I drop the dishtowel and sprint to my bedroom. Once I've closed the door and am in the far side of the bathroom, I collapse to my knees with heavy sobs.

I allow myself a few minutes of release before I hear the voice of my mother that lives in my head telling me to stop and pull myself together. I drag myself up. The mirror above the sink reflects my swollen red face. As I swipe away the tears, I catch sight of Bob out of the corner of my eye. I didn't hear him enter. I peek at him and then look down, uncomfortable and embarrassed. I don't want him to notice my tears. I don't want anyone to see me cry or be vulnerable like this. When I was little, my family nicknamed me *Puddles* because there were days I would cry a lot. One time my dad put a large pot under my chin to catch my tears while my family stood in a semi-circle and watched, which left me mortified and ashamed of myself. I got the message that crying was not tolerated in our family.

"I heard you." Bob steps towards me and folds me into his arms. I let him hold me even though he's just come back from a run and doesn't smell so good. What's a little sweat when compared to being nurtured, a quality in scarce supply right now? I relax into the comfort of his gentle, strong arms.

"Thank you," I whisper as I straighten myself up. "I've got to get back to the kitchen and finish unloading the dishwasher."

"Are you sure you're okay?" Bob's hazel eyes are soft with compassion. He's still holding me.

"Yes. I'll be fine." I pull away, then lean in and kiss him. He releases his hold.

I trudge back to the kitchen, pick up the towel I had flung to the floor, get a clean one from a drawer, and grab a damp glass from the top rack of the dishwasher. Dishes may not seem like a big deal, but when you've been felled by grief, every small step forward is huge.

This has been a strange morning.

A precursor, I'm certain, of worse to come.

———

DECEMBER 30, 2004

Tsunami deaths now top 117,000. The news gets worse every day, every hour. There's never been anything of this magnitude during my lifetime, and the loss of life is incomprehensible. Some people have lost everyone they love and are now left alone in a country filled with floods, increasing bodies, no clean water, and the potential for many thousands more deaths. I cannot even begin to fathom the level of personal devastation. On this journey with my mother toward her death, I feel even more tuned in to the plight of these people. I imagine myself in their position and the terror they must have felt as they were either swept to their deaths or as they watched those they love disappear. During my years of grief counseling, I've spoken to only a few people who've never found the bodies of their loved ones, and there is a terrible, unresolved quality to their pain.

———

JANUARY 14, 2005

The paper this morning reported that the tsunami death toll is now at 170,000.

Mom and I talk about the tsunami and ache for those who died and all the people left to grieve. We can't imagine the agony of those people who have lost every generation of their family. Even with death not very far from our own lives, we know we are fortunate that we still have time to say "I love you." I tell Mom I love her every day, and she always responds in kind. I've waited my whole life for Mom to say she loves me without my having to say it first. I'm not sure why I feel this way, but it seems like it would mean more if she said she loved me all on her own. I hope she does before she dies.

Chapter 25:

Caregiver Blues

I didn't know then what I know now—that caregiver burnout is real and that the stress of caregiving comes on like a full-frontal assault.
—Nancy L. Snyderman, M.D.,
AARP The Magazine, October/November 2013

JANUARY–MAY 2005

My mother drives me crazy because she's dying and fights me every day on almost everything. She drives me crazy because of how I react to her, and the guilt I feel afterward drives me even crazier.

I feel like an imposter when anyone says I'm a wonderful daughter for taking care of my mother. My mean inner voice says things like: *You should do better, be more patient and understand-*

ing. With your career, you should know better how to care for a dying person. You shouldn't have negative feelings about your mother. You're not a good daughter, no matter what anyone says. I expect more from myself than I deliver. I think I need to be a saint and "should" be perfect in every interaction with my mother. Each time I'm abrupt or irritated, I tell myself it's not okay—I'm not okay. It's a terrible dilemma, and it won't end any time soon.

I would never speak to friends or clients the way I do to myself. I'd tell them they are doing the best they can, and I would understand if they were sometimes short and impatient—watching someone we love wither away wears on us. If I were with a client, I'd recognize the signs of burnout I can't see in myself.

The habit of believing I'm not being good enough didn't begin this year or even last. It's been nestled inside me since childhood, when my dad expected a fearless daughter and met anything less than an "A" on my report card with a fire of angry words. It comes from all the times I was told to "stop crying or I'll give you something to cry about," and being nicknamed "Puddles," and from every time I was punished for not being perfect, although I was never told what that meant until I got something wrong.

My job in the family was to be the cute, sweet, good girl. When I was twelve and my father died without warning, I was certain it was my fault. The fairy tales I loved all promised that if you were a good girl, you would be rewarded with good things happening to you. I reasoned I must have been very bad or my dad wouldn't have died and Peter wouldn't have become increasingly violent with me. Dad's death was my punishment. And now, so many decades later, I carry those early messages telling me I'm not good enough. I thought I'd put them to rest in therapy, but like the ghosts in the horror film *Poltergeist*, "they're heeere."

The months blur one into the next with a stifling sameness. The process of Mom dying begins to suck the vitality out of my own life. I feel like that Charlie Brown character who walks under a cloud. I no longer enjoy anything I do, and even when I laugh, it's shallow and never reaches that wonderful place inside that feels like a tickle. It's like Mom and I are on a nonstop conveyor belt where the progress forward is measured by Mom's physical decline, which wears me down, and I can't find my way to joy or happiness. I know for sure that there's no joy to be found where we're headed. Mom has been given a death sentence as surely as if she were a convicted criminal, but we don't know the date of her execution. I try to manage my moods and exhaustion, and I'm more sleep deprived than normal, even for me. My insides are knotted like an overbaked pretzel, but I must keep up with this somehow. I struggle to find some peace, or sleep, or something to look forward to. If I don't, I won't be much good for Mom either.

We are like a couple looped in a never-ending dramatic play:

The War of the Pills—Plays in the Kitchen Three Times a Day, Seven Days A Week

"I took them." She sounds like a petulant child.

"No, you didn't." My voice comes out harsher than I intended.

"Ginni, I did." She crosses her arms and glares at me. Her tone is ugly; the *I'm your mother pulling rank* voice from my childhood.

The sound is like a red flag waved in front of my eyes, and I react like a bull. I know I'm overreacting again, but I can't help it.

Sounding impatient I say, "Mom, if you'd taken these pills they wouldn't be in the container. Look." I point to the pills nestled in their translucent purple slot. I'm trying to stay in some kind of control despite feeling exasperated.

"Well," she snarls. "Fine. Give them to me." She thrusts her hand towards me.

I give her a glass of water and tilt the pills into her bony hand.

"I hate water." The way she curls her lip and scrunches her nose you'd think I was forcing her to drink sewage.

"I know you do." I manage to sound neutral.

She tosses the pills into her mouth, sips a small amount of water, and clunks the glass down onto the kitchen counter. With a last glare my way, she turns and leaves the kitchen.

Mom never capitulates without an argument, leaving me exhausted and strung out like I've walked across a canyon balanced on a shaky thread.

We are locked into an ancient tug-of-war: a mother-daughter struggle for independence and power. Our roles are switched from when I relied on her for everything then grew into a petulant teenager determined to pull away and make my own decisions. Mom's tones—the same ones that used to raise my blood pressure—now come out of my mouth when I speak to her. I didn't like it in her and like it even less in myself.

I try to be pleasant, but I hate the situation we're in. My neck and shoulder muscles are tight and my head throbs.

I'm petrified she will die after incidences like this, when the spaces between us loom large. The last words between my father and me were said in anger, and for years I was haunted by guilt and regret. I want the last words my mother hears from me to be a gentle *I love you*, and I hope those are her last words to me.

We have a ways to go.

⁓

Thursday Matinee—Plays Once A Week

I drop everything and leave my office so I can be home by 10:45 in the morning to take Mom to her beauty appointments.

"Mom, time to go," I call out as I enter the house. Sunny and Sophie rush up to me, and I can't help but smile at the sight of their smiling faces and wagging tails.

Mom is behind them. Her left hand grasps the handle of the oxygen dolly and her purse is slung into the bend of her right arm.

"Do I need this?" She nods towards her purse, her voice sweet as a child's.

"No, you don't need it." I used to be irritated with her for asking. Irritated because she's confused. It's painful to see my once self-assured mother unable to recall something as simple as whether she needs her purse. I'm tired of the repeated conversations. With weekly practice, I train myself to be patient. I no longer shake my head or add, *I tell you this every week.*

She holds out her purse, which I drop on the chair behind her.

As we drive the five minutes to the beauty salon where she will get her hair and nails done, I ask if she'd like me to take her to Sammy's or Ruby's Diner when she's done.

"Sammy's." She smiles. When she smiles, I feel like the good girl I want to be.

After I park the car, I drag out the heavy oxygen tank, then help Mom out. She's on her feet and off in a hurry before I can shut the door and lock the car.

When I catch up to her, I find Mom standing in front of the

glass door to the salon with her hand on her chest. "I ran out of breath," she gasps.

I won't allow her to see me crumble as I struggle not to cry every time this happens. I maintain the stoic façade Mom taught me so well.

"Mom, you've got to slow down."

"I can't help myself. I walk fast."

"But then you have trouble breathing." My words are a challenge but my tone is plaintive.

"I don't know how to walk slow." Her posture straightens and her chin tilts up with pride.

I used to argue with her about this, but I've learned there's no point. I open the door and follow her into the waiting room filled with the aroma of shampoo and hairspray. Once she's seated and I let her hairstylist know we're here, I leave for my office, ready to attend to urgent business in the couple of hours I have free.

No Way Out—Plays One Afternoon Only (Thankfully)

Worse than the daily war of the pills arguments or weekly breath-taking race to the beauty salon is the afternoon I enter the kitchen and find Mom frozen like a statue in front of the counter, hand on her chest. Sunny and Sophie are sitting by her side, looking up at her.

"Mom, are you okay?"

She shakes her head.

I race to grab her nebulizer, put it into her mouth, and push the pump. She inhales. Her blue eyes are dark, sunken orbs.

"You couldn't breathe? Couldn't catch your breath?"

She indicates *no* with another small headshake and holds up her index finger to signal I should wait.

After a few minutes that feel more like an hour, she says, "I could inhale but I couldn't exhale."

"Do you need the Advair?"

"No." She pauses, then adds with a slight waggle of her head, her voice a pensive, wistful whisper, "I can't believe it's gone so fast."

She means her life.

I remain silent. What can I say? I'm not ninety with a terminal illness, and any philosophical comment would be empty words. I give my mother my presence, the only useful thing I have to offer. I allow her to be where she is with no need to try to fix what I can't. This appears to be enough.

She thrusts her chest out and says, "I'm okay now. I'm going to my room."

"I love you, Mom." I somehow manage to hide the chokehold of sadness around my throat.

"I love you too."

She walks out of the kitchen with my two golden girls tailing behind her. I'd like the girls to be with me but Mom needs them more. On Mom's worse days, they never leave her room.

After she's gone, I suck in a deep breath and try to let it out while forcing myself to keep it in. I want to understand what Mom had experienced. Within seconds, I am uncomfortable. When I'm an inch away from panic, I release my breath, grateful I can still choose to breathe. My mother's body has robbed her of that choice.

She might have died if I hadn't chanced into the kitchen when I did.

I'm beyond numb.

———

Dead or Alive—Plays Two to Three Times Daily

I stand at the doorway to Mom's room. She's lying on her side faced away from me, her body still. Time stops while I watch for any movement, wondering if she is dead. My jaw clenches and I can't breathe.

After what seems like an eternity trapped in Dante's Inferno, her back rises and falls. I take a breath and relax, relieved. She's still alive this time, but I know I'll continue to reenact this heart-stopping moment every day and night until she dies.

I go to my room to recuperate. On the king-size bed I feel small and insignificant in the face of all I have to do to keep my mother alive. I stare at the blank TV screen. I can't catch my thoughts and barely notice tears on my cheeks. I'm lost but have to act like I know what I'm doing. I must be good at pretending, because none of my friends, colleagues, or Bob have noticed that I've disappeared.

I want this to be over. No! How can I think that? "Over" means Mom will be dead. I want it over because I'm no longer certain I can outlive her. I'm that weary, worn, and tattered. I can't tolerate watching and waiting every day. I'm appalled by my thoughts for it to be over. I don't share this with anyone, not even Bob, because I'm sure he'd break up with me once he knew what a horrible person I am.

I think I'm still able to handle things well enough, but our reality is probably more like the scene in Superman when they're flying and he tells Lois Lane not to worry because he's got her. She looks down and wonders who's got him.

MARCH

When I can't take the stress any more, I call the Riverside County Office on Aging to learn about their services. To my relief, they offer me six free respite days. I take advantage of three of those days and fly to Dallas to celebrate Bob's birthday. Mom encourages me to go, wants me to go, and says everything to reassure me she'll be fine and there's no reason to feel guilty.

She doesn't complain when I take her to Vista del Sol, a health care facility in Rancho Mirage. We're both relieved to find that her room is close to the main desk, faces out on a garden, and she won't have a roommate. Everyone we meet is friendly and assures me they'll take good care of my mother while I'm gone. Hospice workers will also visit.

The pleasure of being away and seeing Bob celebrate with his friends—where I enjoy an evening of stories and laughter—is a dim haze that only lifts the pall around me temporarily. I carry Mom with me. I phone her at least four or five times a day, and am relieved by the cheerful tone in her voice.

"How are you doing?" When she doesn't respond, I add, "Breathing?"

She laughs. "Yes, I'm alive."

She's still got her wry sense of humor, knowing full well I

mean her ability to breathe. Breathing, after all, is the issue now because of her congestive heart failure and emphysema.

"Don't you have something better to do than call me?"

I laugh. "No, Mom, nothing better to do."

"Of course you do. Now go and have a good time."

She sounds content. I pray that she will be alive when I come home.

A few days after my return we're back to our normal struggles, and any peace I found in Texas melts away like a mirage.

A week later, I join a caregiver's group, which gives me a place to vent all my frustration and fear. Mom's stubbornness and opposition to most of what I say and do infuriates me. I'm worried she'll die after one of our arguments—not that I think arguing would kill her, but I don't want to be left with the memory of our last moments together being unpleasant. I want our last conversation to end with the words "I love you."

Every woman in this caregiver's group is also coping with an elderly parent. We are all frayed. These strangers are my comrades-in-arms and offer me compassion and understanding. Their eyes are sympathetic as they say, "You're a good daughter"; "Your mother doesn't sound easy"; "You're doing the best you can." I'm relieved to realize I'm not a she-devil of a daughter.

Some share that their parents always say "thank you" and tell them how much they appreciate what they're doing for them. I'm jealous because my mother has rarely thanked me in all the years she's lived with me. We might get along better if she let me know she appreciated me. Maybe then I could let myself off the hook for being less than perfect.

Most of the ladies have trouble with other family members and reveal intense hostility towards siblings who don't help and never express any gratitude for all they do.

My half-brother Peter has been out of the picture for so long I don't even think of him as someone I could call on, but hearing these women express their anger reminds me how furious I am that he has not been there for his mother.

He didn't call her for more than two months after he learned she was in hospice care. He had to realize what hospice meant. Could he be that cavalier about his mother's life? I should have expected he'd be like this. Six years ago, when she first got sick and almost died, he said, "I've gotten used to the idea my mother will die. What bothers me is the aftermath."

I thought he would at least try by now to offer something, although I don't know why I held on for so long to the hope he'd be there for Mom. I no longer have that hope.

I'd hate him if I weren't so tired.

———

MAY

Despite all the frustration, my short temper, exhaustion, sleepless nights, and struggle to keep my nonprofit center alive through all of it, I am slow to admit I'm not doing as well as I think.

I'm in my home office, seated in front of my computer, my mind an unfocused blur, when an image of me as a juggler appears. The three balls represent my mother, my Center, and my life. I toss them up, but instead of staying aloft, each ball drops to the floor, flattens out like Dali's *Melting Clocks*, and lies immobile at my feet. What I couldn't admit to myself before is now clear: I can't go on or everything will be lost. I've got to find someone to take over my Center, and hospice is no longer enough help here at home.

The next morning I call Sandra, the hospice social worker. "Sandy, I feel like I'm coming apart in pieces. I can't take care of my mother anymore. I'm about to collapse, and I worry about what will happen to us both as her health continues to decline. I'm terrified I won't be able to help her when she needs me the most. I can't keep doing this alone."

Sandy offers no assurance that hospice will be there when the end is near. This is not the hospice I'd read about in the journals and books, where the teams moved in and took care of everything. This hospice team had left me with morphine to administer without clear instructions. I tremble at the thought I might not give Mom enough morphine and she'll writhe in pain, or I'll give her too much and I'll be an unwitting murderer.

Sandy faxes me a list of homes that provide full-time care to people at the end of their lives. Sandra says my mother will be very angry and might even hate me for a while when she finds out.

I'm scared but I have to take the risk. I've reached a boundary of what I am able to do. I read the list while I pet the dogs, then I call Bob for moral support.

Chapter 26:

The Search

Wave of Sorrow,
Do not drown me now
　　　　　—Langston Hughes

MAY 2005

I never imagined we'd be in this position. Mom and I always assumed she'd go fast, like my dad and her brother. She was also wrong about her age, thinking she would die when she was eighty. "I never want to be a burden on you," she used to say. But that was then, before her body started the betrayal all old bodies do. When a sudden medical crisis made her vulnerable, she was forced to rely on me, but soon after she moved to the desert she returned to her vibrant self, and we forgot she had almost died or how frail she'd been. We renewed our belief that when death arrived some day in the far away future, it would come with no warning. We carried this delusion until she got to where we are now, a point of no return.

Because Mom and I never discussed the possibility of her moving, I feel like a snake in the grass as I drive to Casa Contenta, the first licensed board and care assisted living home on Sandra's list and the one she said was the best. They expect a bed will be available within two weeks. I'd contacted every name Sandra suggested and they all were expensive, $3,500 to $4,000 a month to start, plus an extra $500 a month because Mom is with hospice, and another $250 if she ever needs a hospital bed. I asked but none of them explained why they would charge more for hospice. I hope to find a way to get them to agree to waive the extra hospice and bed fees. Thirty-five hundred dollars is a lot more money than we can afford, but if necessary I'll spend my last penny.

Casa Contenta, a large beige home in Rancho Mirage, is pleasant enough from the outside, but once inside, the stench of sickness and decay mixed with Lysol take me back to my days on the hospice ward. The low popcorn ceiling and bland linoleum floors add an institutional ambience to this converted home.

A petite woman in oversized hospital scrubs lumbers towards me. When I introduce myself, she points to a tattered olive green couch in the living room and tells me to wait. A large man with wavy white hair, spotted skin, and a cannula in his nose reclines in a chair next to the couch and watches a silent TV. He doesn't acknowledge my hello. The whir of his oxygen compressor reminds me of Mom, and I fidget when I envision her at home, innocent of how her life is about to change. Someone down the hall moans, and a round-shouldered woman bent over a walker shuffles past me and through a door, where she disappears like a wraith.

I have that icky feeling I get when I know something is wrong. I stand up, grab my purse, and am about to leave when a chunky woman with frazzled, pale hair calls my name.

"I'm Mrs. Jackson, the administrator. Come with me."

I follow her down a wide hallway and we stop at the door of a cheerless room with three twin beds. Heavy drapes cover the windows, and the room is as dim as the sky at dusk.

"On the phone you told me you had a private room available."

"No, not yet. In a month or so."

"Will it have its own bathroom?"

"No. None of our rooms do, but the bathroom is only a few short steps away."

She walks out of the room and opens another door to a tiny, mustard-yellow bathroom with a sink, toilet, and bathtub/shower combination behind an old shower curtain.

My jaw tightens. There's no chance I'd bring my mother here. She'd hate this, and I wouldn't blame her if she hated me. I'm astonished that Sandra said this is the best of all the facilities on her list. I shudder to think what the other places are like.

"Mrs. Jackson, thank you for your time, but this won't do." I say good-bye and trot out the door, where I'm assaulted by the harsh, hot sun.

The next three facilities are equally abysmal. I'd no sooner move my mother into any of them than I would throw her into a medieval dungeon. I return to my office and bury my face in my hands, tears oozing out in spite of myself. I remember to breathe. The in-and-out motion soothes, like gentle waves rocking a cradle. Once I'm calm, I phone Sandra and complain about what I've seen.

"The only one left on your list is Villa de Consuela. I know you said you wouldn't recommend them, but you refused to tell me why, and I'm going to give them a call."

"Well . . . it's your choice. I'm interested in knowing how it goes." Her voice sounds tense.

After we hang up, I call and a cheery woman answers, "Villa de Consuela, Joan speaking."

"Hi, Joan. I'd like to speak to the owner or administrator."

"I'm the owner."

I explain to her what I'm looking for.

"Well, a single room with its own private full bathroom should be available in about a week or so."

"How much will it cost?" I expect her to quote an outrageous amount since those shared rooms at the other facilities were so pricey. I hold my breath as I wait for her answer.

"Would $2,000 a month be okay?" Her tentative voice suggests she's new at this.

"That would be fine," I say in a neutral tone as I do a little jig out of relief—the price is so much lower than all the others. "My mother is with hospice. Do you charge extra for that?"

"Oh, no, nothing extra."

"What if she needs a hospital bed in the future?"

"That's no problem."

"What will you charge?"

"We won't charge you more."

I am beyond relieved. I mentally jump into the air and click my heels. I may have found a place that won't empty my bank account. We make an appointment to meet tomorrow morning.

Villa de Consuela is a white house on a homey, tree-lined street in Palm Desert, only two miles from my home and less than a five-minute drive. I'll be able to visit Mom several times a day. The front door is unlocked and opens to a bright, wide entry hall. The air is fresh and the house silent except for the voices coming from a television in a small den where a woman sleeps in a green recliner.

I stride towards the hall on my left and call out "Hello" in a soft voice so as not to disturb anyone else who might be asleep. An Asian woman with straight black hair emerges from the kitchen.

"Hello, I'm Virginia Simpson and I'm here to see Joan."

"I'm Joan."

"Nice to meet you." We shake hands.

"Okay, follow me and I'll show you the room."

The spacious bright room is at the end of a short hallway. From the double bed, Mom will be able to look out the large window, where she will be treated to a lush yard filled with colorful flowers and fruit trees. The room is decorated with wicker furniture, including nightstands, a six-drawer dresser, and a chair with a soft floral pad in front of the generous walk-in closet. I plan to put her TV on top of the dresser; that way, when she watches her shows, she can glance at the shelf above, where I'll place her favorite photographs. The room is larger and nicer than Mom's room at my house, and the best part is the full en suite bathroom Mom will have all to herself.

"Very nice, Joan."

She smiles. "Let me show you the rest of our home. We allow a maximum of six guests at any one time and provide onsite, trained, certified help twenty-four hours a day, seven days a week. We offer laundry service and three meals a day. If there's any special food you want your mother to have, you can bring it." She pauses with a shy smile, then adds, "But be prepared to share."

"That's fine."

She leads me to a table and points to some papers. "If you don't mind, I need you to fill out these intake forms."

For the first time in days, I'm not burdened by a weight in my heart, and I leave with a spring in my step.

The next day, I call Joan's references. One woman gets snippy when I ask if she would recommend them. "Of course I would," she snaps. "I wouldn't have had my mother there if they weren't good."

"Okay, well, uh, thank you so much for your time." I hang up, relieved to be done with this conversation.

I call Joan and set the date for Mom to move in. Joan promises that if my mother dies before a month is over, she will prorate the cost and refund the money to me. I write out a check for the first and last month's rent.

My next call is to Sandra. "I've visited Villa de Consuela, and I'm going to move my mother there on June 1st. Can you help me find the words to tell her?"

"You should let me do it."

"Why?"

"I've had experience with this, and because I'm not emotionally involved it will be easier for me than for you. I will explain to her why this is necessary, but remember what I told you: she'll probably be very angry and hate you for a while."

"I hope not." My voice catches.

We plan for her to come tomorrow. I want Mom informed as soon as possible so I'll know where we stand. I'm not good at waiting, especially when I'm expecting something that frightens me.

I don't want Mom to hate me. I hate myself enough for both of us right now. I know I'm doing what's best for both of us, but still . . .

I'm worried that I didn't talk to my mother before my search. I thought I'd learned how important it was to empower Mom by giving her choices. After I found Villa de Consuela, why did I allow myself to believe she would hear the news better from Sandra than from me? Was I afraid of her anger or didn't I trust her love for me? Earlier life choices cast a long net over everything that followed, and all those years when she chose Peter over me continue to shroud my belief in her love.

Chapter 27:

Changes

The flower that blooms in adversity is the rarest and most beautiful of all.

        —Walt Disney Company, Mulan

JUNE 2005

Your mother will hate you, Sandra, the hospice social worker, had said. *She will be angry. I will tell her. I know how. She'll take the news better from me than from you.*

Sandra joins me in the living room after she's talked to Mom, and when I ask her how it went, she says, "She understands."

"That's all?" I squint and try to take in what she's telling me.

"Yes, that's all." Although her eyes are warm, the upward tilt of her chin and pierced tone of voice slams the discussion door shut.

I don't understand why Sandra is always evasive or why I never push harder for answers. Time and time again she's shown that once she's spoken, she will not respond to questions or add new information. It's been frustrating to work with her, but now it doesn't matter because Mom's reaction to me will convey how she feels about her imminent move.

After Sandra leaves, I pace while I debate whether to wait or go to Mom now. I envision various scenarios. *I'm at her doorway and when she notices me, she snaps, "Go away! I don't want to talk to you."* Or, *"I'm too angry to talk to you right now. How can you abandon me? I thought I could trust you!"* Or worse, *"I can't even look at you."* Her eyes are hot coals of hatred. *"Get out! I've never been this disappointed in anyone in my entire life. You're a bad daughter."*

With each new thought I feel smaller and more worried until I realize I can't avoid her any longer.

Mom sits on her bed, hands folded in her lap, staring at the TV. She wears a long-sleeve white top with a paisley print and her legs are stretched out and tucked under a lightweight lilac chenille afghan. Her paper-thin skin is no longer sufficient to regulate her body at a comfortable temperature despite the pleasant air-conditioned 75 degrees holding the torrid heat outside in abeyance.

"Mom, can I come in?"

She nods, points the remote at the TV, and mutes the sound. Sunny and Sophie lift their heads but don't move from their spots next to the bed.

I climb over the girls and settle into the space between Mom's feet and the footboard. The back of my neck is damp with sweat.

Before I can speak, Mom says, "I don't want to go." Her voice is a soft, pensive whisper. She punctuates her words with a subtle back and forth movement of her head.

"I know you don't." My voice cracks with a silent sigh and I blink back tears I hope she doesn't notice.

The room appears dimmer, as though someone has lowered the light, leaving us in a gray fog. I fold Mom's hands in mine. I struggle for words but realize there is nothing I can say to make this easier.

Though I'm talking about moving my mother from my house, I can't help but remember that she never threw me out during my teen years, a time filled with conflict I'm certain wasn't easy for her. She never gave up on me, even after some intense arguments.

Our worst fight took place in 1969, six or seven months after she sold my car to Peter over my strenuous objections.

For months I had seethed about her betrayal. One evening, as we sat across from each other eating dinner, I couldn't hold in my resentment any longer and I exploded, saying things like, "How could you have lived so much longer than me and yet know so little about life?"

Mom screamed, "I've had it with your attitude and constant criticism." She slammed her fork down onto her plate, jumped up, and fled the room. We yelled at each other in the kitchen and throughout the house. Mom tried to slam her bedroom door on me and we shouted through the open sliver as I pushed to get in and she kept shoving back to keep me out. I was larger, stronger, and younger, and with one last robust thrust, I forced the door open and bounded into her room. We continued to holler until Mom screeched, "Drop dead!"

I went cold and, without another word, turned away and ran to the safety of my bedroom.

Mom chased after me. "I'm sorry, Ginni. I'm sorry." Her eyes were wide with the knowledge of what she had done. She knew that because I'd told Dad to *drop dead* the night before he died, I was adamant that no one should ever say those words. Our argument ended the moment Mom apologized. We sat close together for more than an hour, both of us sharing what it was like for us to have brothers who hit us. This time Mom listened. When I told her how hurt I was when she didn't seem to care that Peter hit me, and what it meant to me when she'd sold him my car and bought him a new sunroof, she apologized. "I'm sorry, Ginni. I wouldn't hurt you for the world. I'm scared of Peter, too, and maybe I thought I had to sell him your car or risk his anger. When he insisted I buy him a new sunroof, I didn't know what else to do."

Because I understood what it felt like being on the other side of Peter's venom, my heart softened toward her and my anger melted away. I believed we'd reached a new level of understanding.

The day after that fight, in her car on our way to dinner, I told her I was glad we'd had that conversation and how close I felt to her. She didn't remember at first, and then when she did, she said, "Oh, yes. That was when you told me what a shit I was and I took it."

I was too stunned and hurt to respond. I had no fight left in me and deflated with a groan. A huge part of me wanted to jump out of the car and run away from her forever, but I chose to stay.

Mom and I never gave up on each other, regardless of the many times she showed her preference for Peter or my numerous displays of snarky teenage attitude and arrogance.

And now, thirty-six years later, I hope she doesn't believe I've given up on her. I keep my eyes on our clasped hands, afraid of what she'll see in my eyes if I look at her, and even more terrified of what her eyes might reveal. We remain silent for a few minutes and then I look up and whisper, "I love you."

"I love you more." Mom's eyes are soft and their gentleness rips at my guilty heart. She glances at her hands and shifts her position. Her brows are knitted together and she stares at me for what seems like a long time but is probably no more than a minute. I can almost hear the thoughts turning in her mind as she scrunches her face and looks at the ceiling.

"Ginni, I need to ask you something." Her voice is low and solemn.

"What is it, Mom?"

"When the time comes, do you want Peter there?" She doesn't need to say the time she refers to is the end of her life.

I scoot towards her and peer into her eyes. "Mom, this has to be your decision, not mine." I'd like to say, *No way. I never want to be near that S-O-B again.* I don't want Peter within one hundred miles of me—but Mom is the one dying, and I won't impose my wishes on her. She has the right to be in charge of the end of her life. If I must see Peter, I'll make the best of it.

"Thank you, Ginni. I needed to know."

When Mom fiddles with the remote, unmutes the sound, and turns her attention back to the television, I take this as a sign it's time for me to leave. Sunny and Sophie don't stir as I do my best not to trip over them on my way out.

Mom has never moved unless she had to. She was in her seventies when she moved from my childhood home because she couldn't afford the upkeep and needed to live on the money from the sale. She was eighty-five when she moved from her apartment and into my house after her doctor said she could never live alone again. He was wrong. Mom could have lived by herself up until the past year, but at the time, we didn't realize she would recover and do so well for five years. Now she's moving because I say she must.

No one tells me I'm wrong to move Mom. Bob and my friends are supportive and understanding. They each say, *I'm surprised you've lasted so long. I'd never move my mother or father into my home. You've been and are a great daughter.* I view myself as an imposter, and their words bounce off me like I'm made of Teflon. Nagging questions and self-recriminations block out any chance for their support to soothe my conscience. I tell myself I'm not a great daughter. A great daughter would always be kind and patient. In the movie *Dodsworth*, Walter Huston's character says, "Love has to stop somewhere short of suicide." The part of me that recognizes this truth continues to fight with the part of me that believes a great daughter would keep her mother with her no matter what the risk.

My mother doesn't hate me and she isn't angry. She softens into a warm, gentle version of herself and is the perfect houseguest. In all the years she's lived with me she has never touched me except in response to my hug. Now that she's about to move out, she rubs my neck and shoulders with the expertise of a professional masseuse. Her bony hands remember their beauty school training from the 1930s, when massages were one of many skills learned by hair stylists.

Mom is silent while she kneads the knots in my neck and yet I sense her hands saying, *Please let me stay.* I wish I could, but I can't think of any other way to save us. Our life has been beyond difficult, and her staying wouldn't be fair to either of us.

The Thursday before Mom moves, while she's getting her hair and nails done, I visit Talbot's petite store at The Gardens on El Paseo and buy Mom clothes. She hasn't had anything new to wear in a long while and I'm certain seeing herself in these outfits will perk up her spirits. At least I hope so. My purpose in shopping for her is muddled with conflict. I'm not sure whether I do this for her or as a way to soothe my guilt and self-doubt.

WEDNESDAY, JUNE 1, 2005

I'm grateful that Bob flew out to be with me and help move my mother. After he and I fill our cars with Mom's clothes, secretary desk, TV set, and books, we settle her into my car, and Bob follows in his as we drive to Villa de Consuela. Mom is silent and pensive during the two-minute drive. I'm nervous and chatter the whole ride, saying things like, "I'll come visit you all the time, and tomorrow after I take you to your hair and nail appointments, we'll go to lunch." I want to keep reassuring her of my presence and love.

When Mom enters her new bedroom, I scamper around the room to show her what I've done to make everything homey and comfortable for her.

"I've transferred your phone number and bought you a phone with an answering machine so that you'll never miss a phone call from Peter or your friends."

She smiles when she spots her favorite photographs on the ledge high up the wall across from her bed: a large picture of a light-haired, four-year-old Peter; a close-up photo of Mom and

222 THE SPACE BETWEEN

Dad dancing, taken three years before he died; a full-body photo of my chic mother in her twenties, wearing a white hat with
matching white coat and shoes; and nine-year-old me in short-
sleeved cotton pajamas gazing off to the side, cheeks swollen with
the mumps.

She walks over to her bed, sits down, and picks up a small
picture of us taken at a party in 1993. My hair is a mass of curls,
while Mom's looks like the hairdresser stuck a bowl on her head
and trimmed her straight white hair. Her glasses are large but not
as large as my oversized shoulder pads.

"You've always been pretty," she says with a wistful smile.

"You're the one who's pretty, Mom. I always wanted your
blue eyes. That and your thin thighs. Not fair that I didn't get
either," I say with a chuckle, and Mom laughs and opens her eyes
wide, which I decide is her way of showing off their beauty.

We've had this conversation many times since I was old
enough to realize the beauty of her blue eyes compared to my
ordinary brown. Her eyes change colors from sky blue to green
or aquamarine depending on what she wears. They are the mag-
nificent blue and green of the lagoon on the island of Bora Bora,
which is the closest place to Heaven I've seen on Earth. I've always resented that Peter got blue eyes, but I can't recall whether
his change colors. Nothing affects the color of my eyes. They remain dark brown no matter what I wear.

Bob leaves soon after we've settled Mom in and I visit with
her for another hour until she dismisses me with a "You can go
now," and turns on the television.

"Okay, Mom," I say, and lean in to kiss her on the cheek. "I'll
bring you chocolate cake tomorrow."

"Oh, goodie." She claps her hands.

"I love you."

"I love you, too," she says. As I'm about to turn the corner and leave, she tilts her head, and, for a moment, I catch a glimpse of my mother as an innocent, sweet child.

———

Had I known what would occur after she moved, I would have done it years ago. Our relationship alters in wonderful ways as my mother transforms into pure love. Mom's blue eyes, more vibrant than ever, radiate a sweet, gentle kindness and love. She never argues with the staff at Villa de Consuela when they tell her to take her medicine, and she is grateful for everything. She loves the view of the yard from her window, and her attitude reminds me of a haiku I heard many years ago:

Since my house burned down
I now own a better view of the rising sun

Although I'm relieved that Mom has full-time care to tend to her needs, I am still the one responsible for every decision about her welfare. Without our daily arguments over her pills or my needing to be alert at every moment in case she has trouble breathing, Mom and I relax into a new relationship. I get to be her daughter again and I bask in the bloom of her radiant, gentle love.

Chapter 28:

The Blue Wapiti

The nearer people approach old age
The closer they return to a semblance of childhood,
Until the time comes for them to depart this life,
Again like children, neither tired of living nor aware
of death.

—*Desiderius Erasmus*

JUNE–JULY 2005

Mom's move changes our relationship in wonderful ways, but our life together is bittersweet. As much as I enjoy this loving mother, I despise watching her slip away from me as her health declines into one crisis after another.

The second weekend after Mom settled in, Peter and Ellyn stop by on a Saturday afternoon for an hour or so. I wait until Julie lets me know they're gone before I visit.

"How'd it go with Peter and Ellyn?" I nestle into the wicker chair near Mom's bed, a spot I've come to think of as my second home.

"Very pleasant." She smiles with closed lips but there's no glimmer in her eyes.

"I'm glad," I say, but the truth is I think they could and should have spent more time with her.

Mom sighs and her eyes gaze up at the picture of four-year-old Peter. "He was such a sweet child." She deflates a little as she seems to muse about her son. "I don't know what happened to him."

I stay silent. No reason to rehash old history.

She picks up the book lying by her side. Mom has always been a prolific reader but rarely speaks to me about what she's read. She's different now. The book she holds is *Cinderella Man*. She points to the cover photo of a bare-chested man wearing boxing shorts and gloves, and with an excitement unusual for her says, "This took place in my time."

Cinderella Man is the true story of James Braddock, a boxer who lost everything during the Great Depression and needed social aid to feed his family. In 1935, after he won his fight against Max Baer, the heavyweight champion and odds-on favorite, Damon Runyon dubbed Braddock "The Cinderella Man." Braddock never forgot his days on welfare, and after his comeback he returned the welfare money he'd received and made frequent donations to feed the homeless.

Mom's smile is broad and her chest puffs up in the way it always does when she is proud of herself. "I lived during this time." She taps the book cover. "Jimmy and I would go to nightclubs where we'd dine and dance. Jimmy was a great dancer—so was your dad. This was *my* era." The memory of this happier time shines through the energy, enthusiasm, and upbeat, melodic quality in her voice. For an instant her eyes drift into a faraway stare, and I imagine she's seeing herself as a young woman in her husband's arms.

———

The following Thursday, a day so hot it could peel your skin off, I take Mom for her usual nail and hair appointments and afterwards to lunch. Mom wears her new white pantsuit and striped powder blue top. I can tell by the way she stands straighter than usual that she is aware she looks extra pretty. We are on the path towards Villa de Consuela's front door when Mom stops and clutches my arm. Her eyebrows pull together and her smile is crooked, meek, and tentative, a look I interpret as an *I've done something wrong*, little girl smile.

"I couldn't help myself. I peed in my pants." Her tone is sweet as a five-year-old child's yet matter-of-fact.

"I'm sorry, Mom." I search for words to make her feel better but I can't find them, so I act as though it's no big deal. I take her arm and we stride in silence into the house and to her room. Mom grabs a steel blue cotton shift out of her closet and heads for the bathroom to get out of her wet clothes. After five minutes, I ask if she needs any help.

"No. I'm almost done." Her neutral voice helps me relax. A minute later she pops out of the bathroom, climbs onto her bed, and turns on the TV, seeming to be unfazed by it all.

Relieved by her attitude, I ask, "Can I bring you anything? Cranberry raspberry juice?"

"Yes, I'd like that. Thank you."

Mom doesn't seem upset or disgusted with herself, which is unlike her. I'm inspired by her calm acceptance of this new, unpleasant reality. She's always been one to display displeasure when she or others didn't live up to her expectations. This is a new side of the complex woman who is my mother.

I continue to learn from Mom how to grow old and face the end of life with grace. Maybe the lesson is about getting back to the child, to the true essence of the person we were before being molded by our parents and society. She also teaches me about gratitude. My mother is now grateful for everything and enjoys her life. She comments on the beauty of the yard and thanks me for even the smallest of things I do.

———

Liz, who's been our head hospice nurse since last month, stops by twice a week. Liz is an attractive brunette in her early forties. I like her better than Mom's first nurse because Liz is unflappable, competent, and kind. Liz smiles every time she sees me, and unlike Mom's first nurse, never suggests I'm not doing enough for my mother. Four times a week a tiny Filipino woman, also from hospice, arrives to bathe Mom and give her back massages. Mom's hairdresser visits weekly, but her manicurist of six years makes excuses and never comes. Soon I am in a new role with my mother: her manicurist.

"You need to cut your mother's toenails," Julie orders, hands on her hips like a drill sergeant.

"Me?" I can't believe she's telling me to do this. I've never cut my mother's or anyone else's toenails.

"Yes, you." She hands me toenail clippers, turns on her heels, and leaves.

With a playful smirk, Mom pulls her feet out from under the covers and wiggles her toes.

"You enjoying this?"

"Oh, yes." Her eyes sparkle with an impish glee.

"I'm glad one of us is."

I position myself at the end her bed and take one slender, cold foot in my hands. Clipper at the ready, I peer at Mom over my glasses and in a tone flatter than the Texas landscape say, "I've lived for this."

Mom laughs and I laugh with her. Nothing is better than the sound of my mother's laughter, and we've laughed a lot since she moved here. I doubt that I'm funnier than normal, but Mom's attitude is lighter. I've become her personal standup comedienne, and my goal is to make her laugh every day.

With my head close to her feet, I start with her big toe. The nail flies off with a snap. I file it before I move onto the next to smooth any harsh edges that could cut her fragile skin.

Five toes down, five to go, I pick up Mom's other foot and snip the first nail.

"Goddamn you!" Mom yells, her voice an angry, shrill cry.

I drop her foot. "What did I do? What did I do? Did I hurt you?" My heart beats fast.

"Goddamn you for dying young!" I follow her gaze to the picture of her and Dad dancing.

"Oh, Mom, I thought I hurt you." I pick up the dropped foot and continue.

"No, you didn't hurt me." Mom hesitates before adding, "I was criticized when I married your dad so soon after Jimmy died, but wasn't that better than this?"

I nod but say nothing. We both know she means the forty-four years she's spent alone.

Dad's early death altered her life and changed her in every way imaginable. She's different from her friends who lived out their lives with husbands. They maintained their feminine sexuality, and while my mother always cared about her appearance, her manner of dress has been neutral, with no hint of sensuality.

Mom once told me she never cried after Dad died. Maybe she could have allowed love in again if she had grieved.

After I finish my cropping duties, I plop into my chair.

"The thing I'm proudest of," Mom says with a wide grin, "is that two men really loved me."

That's what you're most proud of? I was certain you meant me. Of course, I don't say that. Instead I say, "You were lucky to have known love."

"Yes, I was." She's quiet for a moment. "I think you've found that with Bob."

"I think so, too. I hope so."

———

Bob and I have been seeing each other exclusively for two years and although we never speak of marriage, he loves me enough to sell his house in Texas and move to California to be with me. I hope this means we'll always be together.

The phone is now more enemy than friend. Too often the harsh chime pierces me out of sleep and my heart beats at breakneck speed. I hold my breath as I answer, insides shaking, scared of the words I might hear, frightened the voice will say Mom died while I slept.

Early one Saturday morning, a week after I cut her nails, the phone rings while I'm in bed sipping my morning coffee and scanning the local newspaper.

"You better come right away. Your mother's not doing well." It's Julie, Mom's primary caretaker at Villa de Consuela.

I bolt out of bed and run across the house with Sophie and Sunny. After letting them outside into the oppressive morning heat, I get their breakfasts and call them in. While they eat, I scurry back to my room and get dressed. No time for makeup, and who cares anyway. I grab my purse, jump into my car, and within two minutes I'm at Mom's bedside. I kiss her and tell her I'm here.

She's in a deep sleep that reminds me of patients I've seen on the hospice ward. Each jagged breath jolts her chest, her lungs working hard to allow oxygen in and out. Her coloring, still pink and not the gray of people at the edge of death, offers the one gleam of hope I can hold onto. I park myself in my chair and match my breathing to hers, praying the next breath won't be her last.

Within half an hour, Sandra arrives. She stands at the doorway and gestures for me to come with her.

As we walk down the hallway she says, "All of hospice is on alert. That's what we do when a patient is near the end." Sandra looks at me with compassion.

I stop walking. *Near the end. Already?*

Before I have a chance to speak, Sandra guides me toward the front door. As soon as we're outside, she turns and faces me.

"I want you to see this." She flips to a page in a brown file and points to a form. I recognize Mom's precise handwriting. "Your mother has instructed us not to call her son when she is dying."

I'm stunned. Mom has made a choice I never expected. At the most profound time in her life she has chosen me. My heart expands, and all those spaces inside, emptied by a lifetime of Mom choosing Peter instead of me, fill with her love. I've waited most of my life to believe my mother loves me, and now I know for sure she does. Leave it to her to save the best for last.

I spend the rest of the afternoon seated in the wicker chair watching my unconscious mother. The air-conditioned room is cold, too cold for my cotton shift to provide protection. Goose bumps appear on my bare arms. Sometimes I forget to breathe. I wait and watch. Silent, salty tears drift down my cheeks. Will Mom wake up, or will I be glued to this scratchy wicker chair when she takes her last breath?

An hour after I began my vigil, Mom opens her eyes and says, "I was riding the Blue Wapiti," and then drops back to sleep. I've never heard of a wapiti, blue or otherwise, and assume Mom has seen a mythical creature created in her imagination.

I wipe my face to make certain when and if Mom awakens again, she won't see any trace of tears.

Mom wakes up an hour or so later, looks my way, and in her typical staccato manner says, "Don't you have anything better to do?"

"No, Mom, nothing better." I shake my head and smile.

She closes her eyes and falls back into a deep sleep.

Liz arrives midafternoon. I get out of my seat and greet her.

"How's your mother been?" she asks.

"She's been asleep most of the time. She woke up twice, said a few words, and went back to sleep. Her breathing seems labored."

Liz steps past me and over to Mom's side. She takes her hand and taps it. "Ruth, Ruth, it's me, Liz."

Mom doesn't stir.

With her stethoscope, Liz listens to Mom's chest.

After checking her, Liz leaves to speak with the staff. She returns after a few minutes and tells me there'd been a miscommunication about Mom's medication and she's advised Villa de Consuela to adjust the dosage. Because Mom has slept all day, I assume Liz means they've been overmedicating her. She walks over to Mom, pats her head, and says good-bye.

I return to my chair and stay with Mom until the sky turns navy blue and her breathing has returned to normal. When I arrive at home, Sunny and Sophie greet me at the door, and I bask in their joy and unabashed love. I stroke their golden heads, bend down, throw my arms around their necks, and sob into their fur. Sunny licks my face. Neither girl moves until I stand up, open the back door, and tell them to go out. Later, after I've fed them, I turn on my computer and type the word *wapiti* into the search engine.

I learn that a wapiti is a small Canadian elk. I am fascinated that my mother's blurry brain found an animal from her native country and painted it blue. Blue, the color of the Earth, sky, water, and my mother's eyes.

To my immense relief, Mom recovers and is once again her alert self. I talk to Joyce about her staff overmedicating my mother. She apologies and assures me it will never happen again. I return to my routine of numerous phone calls and twice a day visits. Despite periodic crises over the next few weeks, because Mom always rebounds, I relax into complacency, as though her life will continue with no end in sight.

Hindsight tells me I must have been in denial, the automatic defense that kicks in to help us tolerate the intolerable. We don't choose to be in denial, we're simply there. Denial protects us from taking in more information than we can handle, and when we're ready, it lifts on its own.

I remember the first days after the 1989 magnitude 6.9 Loma Prieta Earthquake. The news told us it wasn't the *Big One* we'd heard about for years. Everyone was on edge, and we worried whether this latest shaking of our world was a forewarning of worse to come. Within two weeks, most of us relaxed and went back to our normal routines. We acted like, or hoped, we would never again experience the ground shaking so strong we had to hold on to something and sit down or be thrust to the floor like rag dolls.

Perhaps emotional blinders are necessary or we would be paralyzed by fright and unable to live our lives because we'd be overly vigilant. Perhaps those kinds of blinders allowed me to get through day after day waiting for my mother's last breath.

Chapter 29:

Have You Been Listening?

Turn your wounds into wisdom.

—Oprah Winfrey

AUGUST 2005

Mom and I are August babies. My birthday is the 12th and Mom's is the 28th. She was born early in the twentieth century, during World War I, and ninety-one years later, America is still at war. I've sung "Let There Be Peace on Earth" since I was five years old, and there's never been a time when we weren't at war with someone.

I sometimes feel I've spent most of my life at war: war with my brother Peter and war with Mom. Those wars are over now. I never see Peter, and Mom and I have resolved the differences between us.

Every day since she woke up in July, Mom has asked, "Are you having fun?" Before I answer she will say, "Have fun. Make sure you have fun."

During my afternoon visit on August 10th, Mom's brows pinch together as though she's deep in thought, and with great solemnity she says, "Having fun, being kind, and loving are the most important things."

I grab a piece of paper and a pen from my purse and write down what she's said to capture and remember her hard-earned wisdom. Her few words will become my guidepost and standard for how I measure each day: *Did I have fun? Was I kind? Was I loving?*

Having fun was never at the top of any of my to-do lists. Mom didn't have much fun after Dad died, and her words make me think she now realizes she wasted too many years being angry and sad rather than finding joy and playing. When he was alive there were parties and laughter, but after his death, her life became serious: she was serious, our home was serious, and I was serious. I have to think back to the years when Dad was alive to find the mother of my childhood whose smiling red lips comforted me when I looked at her. Dad's death stole her smile.

At her deepest core, my mother is a gentle woman who too often came across as hard and sharp. After Dad was gone, she was as fragile as fine crystal and not strong enough to allow herself to be vulnerable. Now she is no longer strong enough to be anything but vulnerable, and the transformation has given her access to a wisdom that eluded her while she was healthy.

She doesn't want that to happen to me. Her words are more than advice on how to live: they are a warning about what I'll miss if I fail to understand that having fun, being kind, and loving are the most important things.

FRIDAY, AUGUST 12, 2005

"Happy birthday, honey," Mom sings out as I enter her room. She opens her nightstand drawer, pulls out a large white envelope, and nudges it into my hand. "Open it."

She watches me open the envelope and remove the card. The front shows a pink, long-stem rose, and although the printed sentiment about being a special daughter is sweet, the words Mom wrote inside mean everything:

> *I love you so much.*
> *You mean so much to me.*
> *You get prettier every year. I*
> *Really lucked out in you.*
> *Your mother*
> *Love you*
>
> *You are so important to me*
> *Your mother*
> *Ruth*

I bend down to hug and kiss her. "That's beautiful, Mom." Although Mom always signs letters *Your mother*, and I always kid her about it, this is the first time she's added her name, *Ruth*.

I wonder if by signing her name, Mom was making a statement that she wanted to be sure she was remembered, and that a woman named Ruth had lived. Perhaps she was seeking recognition that she, Ruth, was a person in her own right, beyond any label of daughter, wife, widow, mother, or grandmother. Ruth was here and she lived.

"How did you get the card, Mom?"

Her eyebrows rise and her limpid blue eyes twinkle like stars. "I have my ways."

I settle into my chair.

"Now, to change the subject . . ."

"Yes," she says, drawing out the word.

"Mom, are you sure you're okay with me going?" We've had the conversation before about my plan to accompany Bob to Boston to join his friends at a charity golf tournament. We're scheduled to leave tomorrow morning and return on Tuesday.

"Yes, go."

"You're positive?"

"I wouldn't tell you even if I wasn't."

"What does that mean? Are you saying I shouldn't go?"

She sits up straight in her bed and leans towards me with fisted hands on her hips. "Have you been listening to me?"

"Yes, Mom, I've been listening."

"How many times have I told you to have fun? Make sure you're having fun. Have fun, have fun, have fun." When she's finished, she rests against her pillow as though the effort to get through to me has depleted her energy.

"More times than I can count," I say with a giggle.

I stay with her until it's dark. I kiss her good-bye and when I reach the door, I glance back over my shoulder. Mom tilts her head to the right and with the grin of an adorable child says, "I love you."

My heart expands and I experience a strong pull to stay with her. I return her *I love you* and force myself out the door.

I can only imagine what Mom is giving up so I can leave with a clear conscience and her blessing. For the past two months, Mom and I have been enjoying every moment we spend together, time filled with meaningful conversations and laughter despite— or maybe because of—the precious few days left before she dies. She knows she's dying, and her time (and our time together) is limited, yet she is willing to go days without seeing me because she wants me to have fun. Is this what she meant all the years when she said *No one will ever love you like I do*? Who else but my mother would sacrifice her happiness for me?

SATURDAY, AUGUST 13, 2005

Bob and I depart for Boston early in the morning. I call before the plane takes off. Julie answers Mom's phone, and when I ask to speak to my mom, she says, "Your mother's shaking her head to say she doesn't want to talk to you right now."

I can't believe Mom doesn't want to talk to me. "What's wrong?"

"Nothing."

"Is she all right?"

"She's fine. Just tired."

"I can get off the plane and be there in an hour or so."

"No need to. Go and have a good time."

I relax a little. "Okay—Tell her I love her."

As soon as we land in Boston, I call again.

Julie says Mom is asleep. For the rest of the day and the next, each time I call, Mom's not available to speak with me but Julie assures me she's all right. Because Julie has phoned me more than once the past two months to say my mother's health is failing and I should get there as soon as possible, I trust she would be honest now and let me know if I should catch the next plane home.

I'm closer to Mom than I ever was to my father, and the day he died I woke up with an odd sense of doom. I'm certain I would know if Mom's death was imminent. Although I am concerned and anxious, I don't have any premonition Mom will die while I'm away.

I call often but Mom is never available to talk. Julie continues to say she is fine and not to worry.

Asking me not to worry is like asking a tornado to stop spinning.

Chapter 30:

The Blue Chip

The cure for anything is saltwater—sweat, tears or the sea.

—Isak Dinesen

The wind and the waves are always on the side of the ablest navigator.

—Edmund Gibbon

SUNDAY, AUGUST 14, 2005

With no warning, clouds form and the sky turns charcoal. Rain and lightning end our practice round and force us off the golf course. We escape into a nearby restaurant for an early dinner with Bob and four of his friends. My cell phone rings just as we're seated at a long table in the empty back room.

I go to the front of the restaurant to take the call from hospice. "Hello," I say, tentative and scared, holding my breath.

"Dr. Simpson? This is Marcia. I'm a nurse with hospice. I just checked on your mother and there's been a change. I'm sorry to tell you—she's dying."

My stomach spasms.

"Dying—I'm in Massachusetts. I'll catch the first flight out."

"Dr. Simpson, you should stay where you are. You've done a lot and you must take care of yourself. There's really nothing you can do here. I promise we'll take good care of your mother."

I've never met Marcia, but she's gentle and kind, and her concern for my welfare is touching.

"No, I'm coming home. How long do you think she has?"

"We can't ever give an exact time, but my experience tells me she's near the end. How near, I can't say. She could be gone tonight, tomorrow, or she might even last another week or so."

After we hang up, I plod back to the table. "That was hospice. My mother's dying." I turn to Bob. "I've got to get back to California."

Bob gets up and takes me in his arms. "I'll start checking on flights." He kisses me on the cheek and leaves the room.

I don't remember all of their words, but everyone at the table starts telling me how I should think and feel. Useless things like, *"Be positive"; "Your mother's old. She's had a good long life"; "You were expecting this."* I do my best to listen and be polite. I realize they mean to help, but their words upset and irritate me. When I'm about to rupture into a flood of tears and scream if I hear one more word, I mumble an excuse and run from the table into the bathroom where I can be alone and cry. I find no comfort in being told my mother is old. What matters to me is that I am losing her. She's the one person I have loved my entire life. And if this isn't being positive, I don't care. I'm hurting and need to sort out my thoughts and feelings.

Barbara, a sweet-faced, heavyset woman with tightly curled short hair, follows me in. "We're just trying to help you."

I want her to leave so I can stop my strong woman act and let the little girl inside me wail for my mother. I realize Barbara intends to soothe me, but her presence scratches at my last nerve.

I use what little energy I can muster to say, in a raspy whisper of a voice, "I know, Barbara. I know everyone means well. I just need some time by myself and then I'll rejoin you."

Barbara hugs me and leaves. Once she's gone, I slip into the cubicle and grab a chunk of toilet paper. I give myself over to the chest-heaving sobs of the child I am whose mother is dying.

———

We're trapped in Boston. The East Coast is a mass of storms and all planes are grounded. Back in our hotel room, Bob phones one airline after another, trying to get us on a flight out. I'm grateful he has taken over and is an experienced traveler familiar with how airlines work.

He's not having much luck.

I sit next to Bob on the edge of the bed in a frightened daze, unable to do more than observe him and listen to his efforts. Will I get home in time? Will I be too late? I repeatedly remind myself to breathe as tears sear my cheeks and slide onto my black golf jacket.

Bob's words float by. "I don't care where the plane goes just as long as you get us close to California." He puts his hand over the mouthpiece, turns to me, and says, "I figure if they can get us to a state near California, we can rent a car and drive the rest of the way."

"Okay," I squeak. Speaking isn't easy when a vise of fear has a chokehold on your neck.

Bob continues his conversation with the shadow on the other end of the phone. After what seems like hours, he hangs up and takes my hand. His hazel eyes are soft with love and concern. I see my pain reflected in them. "All flights tonight have been cancelled. No one knows when or if flights will be able to leave tomorrow. It depends on the storms. I've got us booked on an American West flight to Phoenix and we're on standby with Jet Blue for a flight to Oakland. If we can get on Jet Blue, we'll take a connecting flight in the afternoon to Long Beach Airport, where I'll arrange for a rental car to be waiting for us."

"Thank you." My tears turn to sobs, and Bob pulls me into the comfort and safety of his arms.

⁓

MONDAY, AUGUST 15, 2005

After a fitful night of snatched moments of sleep, the phone rings. The room is dark and I glance at the clock. Five thirty. Bob answers, says yes a few times, and hangs up.

"Ginni, we've got to leave now for the airport. They're still not sure when planes will be allowed to depart due to the weather, but we need to be there and ready when the storm breaks."

Because we packed the night before, we're dressed and on our way in less than five minutes.

⁓

Inside the cavernous, bland terminal is a mass of people standing in long lines. We're headed towards the American West queue when Bob notices there's no one lined up at Jet Blue and pulls me in that direction.

I'm like a sleepwalker. I don't recall how we got there, but as though I've been teleported we're in the air, and I'm sitting in the third row aisle seat directly behind Bob, who's in the second row. The seats are pale gray, leather or fake leather, and more comfortable and larger than even the first-class seats on other airlines.

I'm grateful for the TV monitor on the back of Bob's seat. For the next five hours, I mindlessly watch a show narrated by Robin Leach about the yachts of the rich and famous.

The yachts and ocean remind me of my dad, who loved to fish. When I was nine years old, he became partners with three others in a forty-two-foot boat named *The Blue Chip*. Before long, he was the captain, and the only one of the partners to use and care for her.

I didn't fall in love with *The Blue Chip* the first evening Dad took Mom, Peter, and me to San Pedro Harbor where she was docked. My steps were tentative as I walked down the steep incline. The unstable slip swayed back and forth to the splash of dark, stinky water that smelled like rancid oil. Up and down, back and forth. I struggled to stay upright and still remain close to my family. By the time I got to the back of the slip, Dad and Peter were on board. Dad reached over the water to help Mom. She was game and scrambled right aboard.

"Come on," Dad said to me in his usual gravel of a deep voice.

I stepped forward toward the boat, and as Dad grabbed my arm and I lifted my foot, the boat moved away from the slip and I recoiled.

"Come on." Dad held out his hand.

"I'm scared." Worst words I could ever say to my father, and I should have known better, because he always got angry when I was afraid.

"Get on," he ordered, his face contorted and ugly.

My body shook like aspen leaves in the wind. I peeked up at my father from between my hunched shoulders.

"If you don't get on right now, you're never coming on this boat!" His voice was hard and loud, which was typical for him when he didn't like something. He expected obedience from his children. "Help her, Peter."

Peter jumped off the boat and stood beside me.

I was more afraid of Dad's anger than the threatening water. I gulped and reached my hands towards the side of the boat. As I lifted my foot, the boat shifted away again. Dad grabbed my hands while Peter lifted my legs, leaving my body stretched out like a plank between the two of them. With a sharp tug and a push, *voilà*, I was on.

Not an auspicious start to my sailing career.

After a few more visits to *The Blue Chip*, I got my sea legs and would walk everywhere with sure steps. I pretended to be fearless. I would scamper up the flight of stairs to the captain's mast even when we were out to sea, tossed by ocean water.

The last few months of Dad's life, on Monday nights when Mom played Pan with her girlfriends, Dad drove me down to *The Blue Chip*. We'd sit in the aft and talk in the dark. I don't recall one word of our conversations. Not one, not a murmur, not even a hint whispered in my dreams. I wish I'd known to pay attention. *The Blue Chip* was sold after Dad died, but I never forgot her special place in our lives.

⌒

I stare at my cell phone and inhale a deep breath to gather my courage. My hands quiver and I force myself to turn it on. I'm in a hard chair at the Oakland Airport and Bob is beside me. I wait for the phone to come to life. Will there be a message? Is she still alive? I am more than terrified to find out what may be waiting for me on the other end. *Please be alive. Please be alive.* Tears pool in my eyes ready to spill over.

No messages. I breathe again. My body remains coiled.

I dial Mom's number.

"Hello." It's not Mom.

"Julie, it's Ginni. Is she okay?"

"Yes, she's okay."

"Can I talk to her?"

"Just a minute." The phone makes that sound like paper being scrunched up.

"Hello." Mom's voice is weak.

I swallow my tears and in a calm, steady voice say, "Mom. Hi. I'm so glad to hear your voice. We just landed in Oakland. Our plane to Long Beach leaves in an hour and then we'll rent a car and drive to the desert. We should be there by five thirty at the latest."

"Good."

"I love you, Mom. I'll see you soon."

"I love you too, honey. Hurry."

I gaze at the phone after we hang up filled with a mixture of relief and worry. Relieved that she's alive and we got to talk, but still worried she'll die before I get home. Overhead a voice blares that our connecting flight has been delayed, meaning our plane will get into Long Beach late. I could scream. Bob calls the car rental agency to make certain they will hold the car for us until we arrive.

We catch a small break and the incoming flight arrives only ten minutes late. The Jet Blue people are efficient, and within a short period we are in our seats.

An hour later our plane lands, and as we taxi towards the terminal, I notice a name written in script across the front side of a Jet Blue plane parked to our right. We deplane down a flight of stairs, and when we reach the bottom step, I turn back to see our plane's name: **Blue Chip**.

"Bob!" I tap his shoulder and point. "Our plane has the same name as my dad's boat."

There's a saying that *a coincidence is when God creates a miracle in which He wishes to remain anonymous.* Although I'm not religious, I am certain that *Blue Chip* was our coincidence.

Bob gets the rental car and pulls up to the terminal so he can load our bags into the trunk. He slides in behind the steering wheel, pats my leg, and off we go back to the desert. During the ride, Bob and I are quiet, and I repeat a silent mantra: *Please wait for me. Please be alive.* We are fortunate that the traffic is light, and we get there in just under two hours.

Bob pulls up to my house, where I say good-bye to him, pick up my car, and race to Villa de Consuela. I run down the hall to Mom's room.

To my immense relief, she's seated upright in her hospital bed and looks up with a smile as I enter. I rush to her side. No tears. Even though years ago she gave me permission to cry when she was dying, tonight I don't cry. I want to be as courageous and brave as my mother.

I bend to kiss her and she touches my head.

"What took you so long," she says with a grin.

"Oh, just massive storms on the entire East Coast."

"Some excuse."

We both laugh and I celebrate that Mom waited for me. I don't know how she managed to do it, but she looks and sounds better than I dared hope.

I glance at the phone on the nightstand to check the message light on her answering machine. The indicator is dark. Peter hasn't called.

"Excuse me a minute, Mom, I've got to ask Julie something."

"Okay. Don't be long."

I find Julie in the kitchen washing dishes. "Julie, have you heard from my mother's son, Peter?"

"No. The only time her phone has rung has been when you called. And he has never once called us on our phone to find out how she's doing." Julie shakes her head and snorts. "Where does he live?"

"Some beach—Newport Beach, I think."

"You're kidding. That's close. I thought he lived across the country and that's why he never visited."

"No." My voice is quiet. "I was the one who crossed the country today."

With a huff I stomp back to Mom's room and pause at the doorway to calm myself.

I settle down next to Mom as close as I can get. I wait for Peter to call. He doesn't, and I feel he has lost all rights to my mother and she is mine alone. I don't say anything to Mom. I'm surprised and heartbroken when she says, "I feel like I've been thrown out like the trash."

"Oh, Mom, I'm so sorry. You didn't deserve this. You've been a great mother to Peter. You've always been there for him and loved him. You're a wonderful mother."

"You're so much better than the rest."

I stand up, flatten my hand out about an inch above the floor, and as I step over it say, "Well, the bar wasn't set very high."

Mom giggles and I laugh with her, grateful to enjoy the sound of her laughter.

Chapter 31:

Echoes of Silence

I've begun to realize that you can listen to silence and
learn from it. It has a quality and a dimension all its own.
—Chaim Potok, *The Chosen*

TUESDAY, AUGUST 16, 2005

Sometimes silence says what we need to hear and sometimes it breaks our hearts.

Mom is acting odd. She's awake but not aware. Her vacant, unfocused eyes offer no indication she knows I'm with her. I talk to her anyway, because I'm aware that hearing is the last sense to go, and whether she acknowledges me or not, I am certain my voice reaches her.

She looks good, as good as someone who is almost ninety-one years old, bone thin, and close to the end of her life can look. Still pretty, every white hair in place.

Mom sits up, puts her feet on the floor, and rises off the bed. Given her mental state, I am surprised by the speed and strength of her steps.

"Mom, I'm here. I love you," I say with a slight hand wave.

Her face lacks expression and there's no hint of recognition in her eyes. After she circles the room a few times, she disappears into her bathroom.

I pace while I wait for her return.

Silence.

I check my watch. Five minutes.

"Mom, are you okay?"

More silence. Nothing crashes to the floor and there are no other alarming sounds to indicate she fell or hurt herself. I continue to listen and wait.

Five minutes later Julie enters the room. "Where's your mother?"

"In the bathroom. She's been in there quite a while."

"Have you gone in to check on her?"

"No."

"Why not?" She shakes her head.

"Oh, I can't do that."

"What do you mean you *can't do that*? She's your mother!"

Julie asks a good question. When I was a child, I never gave Mom an ounce of privacy. She'd lock the bathroom door that faced the hallway, and I would enter through the unlocked door in her bedroom. But that was decades ago, and today I am certain my mother would prefer I not see her on the toilet.

"She wouldn't like it."

Julie shakes her head again and stomps into the bathroom. Two or three minutes pass before she escorts Mom out and onto her bed. Mom rolls on her side and is asleep within moments.

Julie leads me to the door. In a harsh whisper she says, "I still don't get why you couldn't go in there and tend to your mother's needs."

"Julie, I understand my mother. She'll let you and the hospice people do and see things she would never accept from me. I know her."

"Hmph," Julie snorts. She returns to my mother and glares at me while she strokes Mom's head. Thank goodness she leaves a few minutes later.

I observe Mom from my place on the wicker chair across from her and reflect on the past year. "Old age is the shits," she said a few months ago after one of the bouts with her breathing. The shits for her and for me.

While Mom sleeps peacefully, I notice signs that she is near the end of her life. Her unopened newspaper lies at the foot of her bed, and the Trader Joe's chocolate bar I bought her before I left for Boston is unopened at the bottom of her nightstand drawer. My mother loves reading the paper, loves keeping up with current events, and adores her chocolate. That she no longer cares about any of these is a strong indication Mom is in a transitional phase and has let go of worldly interests.

I'm curious and want to understand what my mother has been experiencing today. When she awakens, if she is still as altered, abstract, and distant as she's been since I arrived, I'll never find out.

I want to change this. I want her young and healthy again. I want to see her eyes. I would love to hear the sound of her voice saying *I love you, Ginni.* All I can do is watch and wait.

Her silence is a farewell, a good-bye I don't want to hear. A telling that she's on a journey where I can't follow because it's not my time. Her silence is the start of a much larger good-bye. I don't want to acknowledge what her silence says.

Wake up, Mom. Wake up, I keep thinking as I sit with her, but she doesn't wake up. Her breathing doesn't change either. When I'm certain she isn't going to die today, I kiss her cheek, tell her I love her, and leave.

Bob is at the door when I return home, and I walk into the comfort of his arms. The minute they wrap around me, I begin to sob out the details of the afternoon while he stays silent. Because he has had more than his share of heartbreak, Bob understands there are times when words are useless and silence carries the most profound message of comfort.

Chapter 32:

Perhaps Love

Our love was and always will be deeper than any earthly difference we might have had.

—Don Everly

WEDNESDAY, AUGUST 17, 2005

Bob and I leave the house early in the morning and are on the golf course by six thirty. I don't care about playing golf but figure it's better than staying home alone. I assume it's okay to play because someone would have called if Mom's condition had worsened. They know my cell phone number if they need me, and we should be finished and off the course by nine thirty.

When we reach the tenth hole of the Indian Wells Country Club, I turn on my phone and call Villa de Consuela. Julie answers and I ask how Mom is doing.

"She's okay. Sleeping."

"Should I come right away or would it be all right if I get there sometime within the next two hours?"

"Two hours should be fine."

"Do you need me to bring anything? Mom have enough cranberry raspberry juice?"

"She needs Depends."

"Depends?"

"Yes, adult diapers."

"I know what they are. I'll pick them up and be there by ten."

"See you then." *Click.*

I'm anxious and in a hurry to get to the drug store and over to Mom, so I let Bob continue to play while I wait in the cart. He's a good golfer and flies through the next nine holes in less than an hour. The instant his ball drops into the cup of the eighteenth hole, I tell him to hurry.

———

When I enter the house, I sign the guest book. My name is the only one repeated in a long row of names, and I wonder if I'm the only person who visits or if the others never sign in. As I head towards Mom's room, Julie calls my name.

"Hi, Julie. I brought the Depends." I hold out the bag.

"Good. Let's go change your mother."

"When did she start wearing Depends? She was able to go to the bathroom on her own yesterday."

"That was yesterday. Things change, and this is how it is now." She bustles down the hall and I have to chase after her.

Mom is asleep, dressed in her powder blue striped top. She looks peaceful and her breathing is rhythmic and soft.

Julie pulls back the blanket. Mom wears no bottom other than the Depends. Julie removes the adult diaper and turns to me. "You need to help me turn her to her side so I can get this clean Depends around her behind."

With a gentle, swift motion, we shift Mom to her left side and Julie slips the diaper on. When we turn her to her right, Mom groans. This is the first and only time I've known my mother to indicate she feels pain. My mother has remarkable tolerance, and for her to groan means the pain must be considerable. Mom's eyes open and she shoots me a dirty look. I don't take it personally, because I'm sure it's about her physical experience. Her hard expression is nothing like in the movies where the dying person at the end of life gazes upon her family and friends with pure love radiating from her eyes. Julie finishes with the diaper and we roll Mom on her back and elevate her head on two pillows.

I sit with Mom for a few hours, but her condition remains the same, so I head for home. After I've showered and dressed, I try to relax and read a book. I read the same paragraph over and over again, but can't focus. I'm too agitated to think. I tell Bob I'm going to check on Mom and won't be gone long. Bob kisses me and I'm out the door.

Two minutes later, I settle into the wicker chair. Mom is still asleep and her breathing is the same. Within fifteen minutes my favorite nurse, Liz, arrives.

"Do you want me to examine her?" Liz asks from her perch on the bed next to Mom.

I suspect there is no point in checking her vitals, but I nod in agreement.

As she examines her, Liz tells me about the fun few hours they spent together on Saturday.

"I sat on the bed with her and we watched the baseball game on TV. We talked, kidded each other and laughed a lot. Your mother is a great lady."

"Thank you. I think so too." My eyes fill with tears, grateful my mother found a new friend who enjoys her and recognizes she is a special woman.

When she finishes her exam and releases her stethoscope, Liz tilts her head and shrugs, a gesture that says even she is surprised by Mom's rapid decline.

I stay with Mom another half hour after Liz leaves. Her face shows no hint of tension and her breathing is rhythmic—nothing to cause further concern—so it seems okay to head home.

I'm not home long before I have a strong urge to go to my mother. It's four o'clock. I tell Bob I'll probably stay no more than half an hour and then be back in time for an early dinner.

I'm at Mom's doorway and about to enter when Julie calls my name. I turn around and almost bump into her. She touches my arm and looks into my eyes.

"Your mother is dying. She will be dead by midnight."

"Midnight," I echo, trying to take in her words. My stomach spasms and tears trickle down my cheeks. "Why didn't you call me?"

"I'd just dialed your number when you arrived."

I phone Bob and share Julie's words. "I won't be home until she's gone," I say with a heartbroken sigh. I wipe away my tears and dash into her room. The distance between Mom and the door seems to have expanded, as if her bed is at the end of a narrow tunnel.

The change in Mom since I left her is massive. Even if Julie hadn't told me, it is obvious she is actively dying. With each breath, Mom's chest froths and crackles. She is drowning in fluid.

I settle into a chair near the head of the bed. "I'm here, Mom. I love you. It's okay to go. I'll be fine. I love you."

Her chest jerks upward and the liquid in her chest rumbles. I don't want her to wake up and hear the death roil in her chest. Yesterday and most of today, I wanted her to wake up, but not now. Although she can hear, I hope she's floating in an altered peaceful awareness, a place where she feels no pain or fear.

Every once in a while she nods her head as though she's saying *Yes*. I scan the room and wonder if the Mothership is here for her. I believe some one or some thing has arrived to guide her and ensure her transition is peaceful and safe.

Julie bounds onto the bed and straddles Mom's body like a jockey riding a horse. She twists the top of a small vial, inserts the dropper of morphine into Mom's mouth, and squeezes. "I'm not going to let you suffer," she says with forceful determination.

I am grateful Julie is here to watch over her. She does what I would be afraid to do if Mom still lived with me. The morphine will keep her unconscious and may hasten her death, but there's no reason for her to wake up only to languish and suffer. Julie kisses Mom's cheek, climbs off the bed, and with a gentle touch to my arm, leaves the room.

Through tears, I choke out John Denver's song "Perhaps Love," a meditation on love, my way of telling Mom that whenever I think of love, I will remember her.

I repeat, "You're a great mother, a wonderful mother. Thank you for being the best mother."

I tell her I love her and it's okay for her to go, that I'll be fine, though nothing in me feels like I will ever be fine again.

I had always imagined that losing my mother would be easier

than losing my dad—he died young and without warning. All these years, I'd believed what the books about grief told us—that sudden deaths are likely to be harder emotionally than a death that's anticipated, assuming, no doubt, that as you anticipate a death, you adjust to what is about to happen. Losing Mom was supposed to hurt less because we had time together: time for me to grow up, time for us to argue and resolve our issues. And time for us to get to know each other beyond mother and daughter to become dearest friends. Losing her in bits and pieces these last years has been torture for me, and tonight is unbearable. Maybe for some people losing someone when they are old or after a long illness is easier than a sudden death. It's not for me. I now believe there's never a good time to lose someone we love. Age doesn't matter. What matters is that I'm losing my mother, and once she's gone, I will no longer be anyone's child. I've seen this truth in other people I've worked with in my years as a grief counselor, and now I know it for myself: the worst loss is the one we're going through now.

Bob arrives around seven o'clock. "Honey," he says as he enters the room, "I brought you dinner. I'll watch over your mother while you eat."

"I'm not hungry."

"Of course you're not, but you must keep up your strength. You'll need it to get you through the rest of the evening. I've left a salad for you up front."

I don't want to leave my mother, but like an obedient child, I stand up. I kiss Mom and tell her I love her and I'll be right back. I hesitate when I reach the door. "Bobby, be sure and come get me if you see even the slightest change."

"I will."

"Promise?"

"Promise."

Near the front door on a small white table I find a beautiful salad with chicken strips and mandarin oranges on lettuce huddled in a red Italian bowl. I stare at the salad. I'm not hungry. I apathetically force myself to spear a piece of chicken and bring it to my lips. Before I can take a bite, Bob's at my side, his expression bleak.

"Come with me." He heads back towards Mom's room and I follow. When we reach the doorway, Bob turns around, puts his hands on my shoulders and looks straight into my eyes. "She's gone."

For a moment, I'm perplexed. It's seven fifteen, not midnight. We were supposed to have more time.

"Gone?" I don't want to believe it. "Why didn't you come get me?"

"It happened too fast. She inhaled and never exhaled."

For months I've said that my mother would not allow me to be with her when she dies. Because I'd read *Final Gifts* by Maggie Callanan, I knew that often people feel guilty when they leave the room for a few moments and their loved one dies, but sometimes the people we love need us out of the room so they can let go. I was sure this would be true for my mother, but until now I'd wished she would let me be with her.

I rush into the room. Mom's mouth is frozen open. Her chest doesn't move. I kiss her and stroke her hair. "I love you, Mom." I hope she hears me, wherever she is.

Her body is warm, but I sense no hint of the energy that usually remains in the body for a while after death. I'm certain my mother was ready to leave and most of her had departed before she took her last breath.

"Bobby, did she nod while you were with her?"

"Yes. Twice. I wondered what she was seeing or hearing."

Julie appears at the door and checks Mom to verify she's dead. "I'll call hospice. They'll send a doctor to sign the death certificate. They'll also see to it that your mother is transferred to the funeral home where you've already made all the arrangements."

"Thank you," I manage to whisper.

"Do you want to call your brother or do you want me to?"

"You call. I don't want to talk to him."

Five minutes later she's back in the room shaking her head. "I can't believe it. I tell him his mother's has died and he says, 'But we're going to Hawaii in a few days and I already bought the flowers for her birthday and I can't get my money back.'" Julie mimics his singsong voice.

My stomach and jaw tighten in a familiar anger.

"He also asked me to be sure to send him whatever she'd left for him. Well, I won't send him anything. He'll have to come get it himself," she snarls, and with a huff swipes a strand of hair off her face.

"The only thing here is that picture of him." I point to the photograph of the sweet-faced, four-year-old boy.

"Honey," Bob says, "I'm going to go into the other room and call our friends to let them know." He hugs me and leaves.

Julie surrounds me with her arms and we cry together. Her tears are comforting. She holds me for a few moments then pulls away. "I loved your mother and I'm going to miss her."

"Me, too," I sigh. "Thank you, Julie—for everything."

After Julie leaves, I kiss Mom again.

"I love you, Mom. Forever." With no one nearby to hear me, I break into sobs.

My mother's body is an empty container, yet I continue to stare at her, knowing this is the last time I will see her face.

Epilogue

Sorrow makes us all children again—destroys all differences of intellect. The wisest know nothing.
— Ralph Waldo Emerson

I believe that love is stronger than death.
— Robert Fulghum

. . . my mother is a hovering presence throughout my inner landscape . . .
— Gail Caldwell, New Life No Instructions

My mother's father died in 1961, when I was eleven. I was too young to understand why my forty-six-year-old mother said, "Now I'm an orphan." When Mom died I, too, felt like I was an orphan and understood that a young child lives inside us no matter what our age. Without any parents or children of my own, I found myself unmoored from generations before and after, like a boat set adrift.

I'd always had a mother to guide me. Now, when I was faced with the challenge of learning to live as no one's daughter, she was gone and couldn't help me get through this.

I wished I could talk to her and ask how she had survived her own mother's death. I pined for the times she'd rubbed my head and consoled me when I was a sick or hurt little girl. She was always there to fix a bruise with a kiss and to bandage one of my many scraped knees. She taught me how to live in the world, first with little things, like telling me to look both ways when I crossed the street and showing me how to tie my shoes. Because she read to me, took me to bookstores and bought me books, she endowed me with a lifelong love of reading. Perhaps her greatest gift was to teach me to always be curious and never to stop learning. Throughout my life, my mother picked me up when I fell, physically or emotionally. After she died, I felt small and vulnerable. I was forced to learn on my own how to walk through life as nobody's child.

Sunny and Sophie never left my side those first days after Mom died. They were the perfect grief counselors, always ready to give a kiss and let me hug them. They listened while I cried and never offered advice or vocalized any of those mundane platitudes people too often say in their misguided efforts to offer consolation.

As Mom wished, there were no obituary, funeral, or formal celebrations of life. I gave Bob a list of Mom's card-playing desert friends and some of my friends, and he took care of inviting them to the house three days after she died.

Mom's friends were the first to arrive. I only knew Paula, a steel-haired, slender mouse of a woman with a pleasant yet unremarkable face. When Mom could no longer drive and until hospice came into our lives, Paula would take her to the senior center and movies on Saturdays. Mom and Paula had little in common other than empty lives to share through card games and movies. The other ladies were unexceptional in their gray haired ordinariness and blended in my mind. Each mumbled the usual "I'm sorry. Your mother was a wonderful woman," and then huddled together in the living room and never spoke another word to me.

The rest of my guests straggled in, hugged me, and said the typical few words people say at these times (*"I'm sorry"*; *"You were lucky to have your mother for so long"*; *"She's at peace now"*; *"Call me if you need anything"*) then spent the rest of the time chatting with other guests as though they were at a cocktail party. Bob barbecued chicken, and one friend offered to bring a cake but showed up two hours late. By the time Bob was ready to serve the food, most of the guests had left. They were a ragtag group who didn't understand I wanted them there to share memories and honor my mother. I didn't get the opportunity to speak about my mother or have others say a few words. The whole afternoon was disjointed and not what I'd wanted, leaving me feeling empty and off balance. I don't know what I would have done if Bob hadn't been there to affirm how odd the day had been and to hold me after they left.

Mom had arranged with the funeral home to have her cremains (ashes) scattered with no one present, and I assumed this had been done. To my surprise, in December I received an e-mail requesting my signature on documents that would allow them to scatter her ashes and asking if I wanted to be present.

On a foggy, cold morning, with Bob at my side, in a small boat with two strangers, I released Mom into the Pacific Ocean near San Diego followed by a dozen long-stem red roses. I sent her on a journey around the world as I read Rumi's poems "No Wall"—about having the clarity to allow love to remove all edges and separations—and "Night and Sleep," which speaks of the spirit returning to its old home where it is no longer fatigued. I read four short lines by Robert Lewis Stevenson about grateful memories surviving in times of sorrow, and a special poem I'd written for that day about my mother and her love still living inside me.

Since that day, whenever I see the ocean, I imagine my mother floating along the waves as she travels the world. She's been with me as I gazed into the Indian Ocean in South Africa and the Pacific Ocean as I walked along the shores of the northern coast of California.

⁓

In the weeks after Mom died, to my surprise, when the pain of grief would strike without warning like a hard punch to my stomach, I would cry out *Mommy*, a name I hadn't used since childhood. For months I sleepwalked through each foggy day, hobbled like a person missing a vital limb I never realized I'd relied on.

In the book *Who Dies*, Steven Levine says that people in close relationships act like mirrors to each other. Without my mother, I couldn't find the parts of myself only she recognized and reflected back to me. She took pieces of my childhood and life history with her. Only my mother held the memories of me as the baby who would wake up with a smile, the little girl who cried often, sang, and failed her first ballet class because she was too young and thought the purpose of one of the moves was to sweep the floor with her hand to check how much dust remained on her fingers. These memories belonged to my mother, not me. If she hadn't shared hers, I would never have known them. I wonder what other untold pieces of my childhood died with her.

My mother's absence revealed the depth of her love, and I

understood what she'd tried to tell me all those years when she'd say, *No one will ever love you like I do.* Loving me wasn't an option for her any more than she could choose her height or the color of her eyes.

Mom knew me well enough to recognize when something was wrong, and brave enough to speak up even if it meant triggering my anger. In my mid-twenties, she saved me by reaching out and pulling me back from the abyss with some gentle words of advice. "Ginni, I see you withdrawing. I know what you are doing. I did the same thing, and there comes a time when you can't go back. I don't want you to do that." I recognized what she was saying because I'd witnessed her fold into herself after Dad died and remain inside that self-imposed, isolated place. I didn't want that for myself but wouldn't have known I was doing the same thing if my mother hadn't been there to guide me with her wisdom.

My mother and I weren't perfect, yet throughout our struggles we managed to stay together. Although death took Mom's physical body, it couldn't rob us of our love and relationship.

Conversations with my mother continued in my mind daily after she was gone. I wish *You're Wearing That?*, Deborah Tannen's book about mother-daughter communication, had been written while my mother was alive so that I would have recognized how I misinterpreted Mom and too often took her innocent comments as a criticism when she meant to compliment me. One time I asked her why she paid so much attention to Peter and not me after Dad died and she said, "I knew you were strong and he wasn't." I answered, "But I was twelve."

After she died, I realized she meant that she believed in my courage and strength. Without her personality to get in the way, I understood my mother in ways I couldn't while she was alive.

I began to chastise myself with shoulds and regrets as I grap-

pled with all the times I'd responded with anger instead of kindness. I had to stop my inner dialogue in which I cast myself in
the role of the not-good-enough daughter to my sweet gentle
mother. Twenty-twenty hindsight is clear, and while I wish I had
been more patient and compassionate, I reminded myself that my
mother wasn't always an easy person. It is too simple to rewrite
history in favor of the dead person, and that's never a good thing.

One day, in a moment of deep reflection and sadness about
the too many times I was brusque, I said, "I'm sorry, Mom."

I heard her voice: "Don't be! I was the perfect annoying
mother and you were the perfect annoying daughter."

Within such balanced perfection, we closed all gaps that
separated us.

The last hours of my mother's life, I shared the depth of my
love through the song "Perhaps Love." I recognized the truth in
the lyrics that love was many things: storms, open doors, conflict,
gentle fires—and that no matter how long my life, my memory
of love would be of my mother.

Two years later, as a way of having my mother with us, the
harpist played "Perhaps Love" when I walked down the aisle to
marry Bob.

Acknowledgments

I didn't do it alone, and I am grateful to the following:

Dr. Linda Joy Myers, President of the National Association of Memoir Writers, writing coach, and author of *Don't Call Me Mother*, provided insightful edits, encouragement, and gentle guidance. Thank you, Linda Joy, for pushing me to go deeper and for believing in my story. Kathryn Mattingly, author of *Benjamin*, *Fractured Hearts*, and *Journey*, was a great cheerleader, asking questions and offering helpful suggestions, edits, and support throughout. The late Steve Grossman, author and teacher, was the first to believe in me back in 1978 when I was too insecure to believe in myself. In 2010, I discovered Tammy Coia, The Memoir Coach, in Palm Desert, and found a safe place to share my writing. Jennifer Lauck, *New York Times* best-selling author of *Blackbird* and *Found*, offered brilliant instruction and editing, taught me how to write a scene, and gave me many opportunities to learn to accept writing criticism as a gateway for learning.

I am indebted to those who generously read and commented on my work, without whose support and cogent comments the writing of this book would have remained a dream: Dr. Laura

Lee Summers, Dr. Denver Coleman, Barbara Miller, Suzy Pafka, Marcelle Tudhope, Mani Feniger, author of *The Woman in the Photograph,* and Lynne Spreen, author of the award winning *Dakota Blue.*

I am fortunate and beyond grateful for my oldest and dearest friends, Barbara Miller, Dr. Denver Coleman, Theresa Coleman, Georgia Farinella, Marcia Kaye, Evelyn Hall, Leslie Schwartz, Dr. Julie Madsen, Claire Sanders, and Sunny Evans: You have traveled with me for many decades of my life, believed in me, encouraged me, and have loved me no matter what. You are the best. Thank you for encouraging me to keep writing and for all the great conversations, laughter, and unwavering, unconditional love.

I have to thank my Golden Retrievers, who were with Mom and me, and are now with Mom: Maggie, 1988–1999: Sunshine (Sunny), 2000–2012; and Sophie, 2000–2009.

And most of all, I am grateful for my husband, Bob, a loving, gentle soul who came into my life and stayed. I can't find enough words to tell you how much I appreciate your love, friendship, and support while my mother was dying and throughout the years of writing this book. Who else would listen to me read each chapter, often more than once? Thank you for the best part of my life. I love you with all my heart and more with each passing day . . .

Appendix

General Information on Caregiving

AARP
www.aarp.org/caregiving
Online community:
888-OUR-AARP
877-342-2277 (Spanish)

ARCH Respite Network
www.archrespite.org
Locates programs and services that give caregivers a break

Eldercare Locator
www.eldercare.gov
800-677-1116
Connects caregivers with services and resources for older adults or adults with disabilities

Family Caregiver Alliance—National Center on Caregiving
www.caregiver.org
800-445-8106
www.strengthforcaring.com
Information, education, and services for family caregivers. Includes Family Care Navigator, a list of services and assistance state-by-state

Leeza's Care Connection
Leezascareconnection.org
Provides free services and resources for family caregivers

Medicare Made Clear
Blog.MedicareMadeClear.com/caregivers
Caregiving experts post topics geared to help and support caregivers

National Alliance for Caregiving
www.caregiving.org
Coalition of national organizations that focus on family caregiving issues

National Family Caregivers Association
www.caregiveraction.org
Information and education for family caregivers, including Caregiver Community Action Network, a volunteer support network

National Clearinghouse for Long-term Care Information
www.longtermcare.gov
Information and tools to plan for future long-term care needs

Social Security Administration
www.socialsecurity.gov
800-772-1213
Information on retirement and disability benefits

Strength for Caring
www.strengthforcaring.com

For Services at Home

Meals on Wheels Association of America
www.mowaa.org
888-998-6325

National Adult Day Services Association
www.nadsa.org
877-745-1440

Information about Senior Facilities and Residences

Center for Excellence in Assisted Living
www.theceal.org
703-533-8181

The Green House Project
www.thegreenhouseproject.org
For more than twelve years, transforming institutional long-term care by creating powerful, meaningful, and satisfying lives, work, and relationships

The National Consumer Voice for Quality Long-Term Care
www.theconsumervoice.org
202-332-2275

Leading Age
www.leadingage.org
202-783-2242

For Help Locating Professionals

**National Association of Professional
Geriatric Care Managers**
www.caremanager.org
520-881-8008

National Senior Citizens Law Center
www.nsclc.org
202-289-6976

Information on Hospice and
End of Life Care

Association for Death Education & Counseling (ADEC)
www.adec.org
847-509-0403
One of the oldest interdisciplinary organizations in the field of dying, death and bereavement

Compassion & Choices
www.compassionandchoices.org
Nonprofit dedicated "to helping everyone have the best death possible." Offers free consultation, planning resources, referrals, and guidance

Hospice Foundation of America
www.hospicefoundation.org
A nonprofit that provides leadership in the development and application of hospice and its philosophy of care

National Hospice and Palliative Care Organization
www.nhpco.org
703-837-1500
877-658-8898 (Spanish)

Recommended Reading:

Callanan, Maggie and Patricia Kelly, *Final Gifts: Understanding the Special Awareness, Needs, and Communications of the Dying*

Gawande, Atul, *Being Mortal: Medicine and What Matters in the End*

McLeod, Beth Witrogen, *Caregiving: The Spiritual Journey of Love, Loss, and Renewal*

Morris, Virginia, *How to Care for Aging Parents, 3rd Edition: A One-Stop Resource for All Your Medical, Financial, Housing, and Emotional Issues*

Poo, Ai-jen, *The Age of Dignity: Preparing for the Elder Boom in a Changing America*

Smith, Harold Ivan, *Grieving the Death of a Mother*

Tannen, Deborah, *You're Wearing That?: Understanding Mothers and Daughters in Conversation*

Tolstoy, Leo, *The Death of Ivan Ilych*   •

Yolandes, Angelo E., *The Conversation: A Revolutionary Plan for End-of-Life Care*

About the Author

Virginia A. Simpson, Ph.D., FT is a bereavement care specialist and Executive Counseling Director for hundreds of funeral homes throughout the United States and Canada. She is the Founder of The Mourning Star Center for grieving children and their families, which she ran from 1995 to 2005, and author of the memoir *The Space Between* (She Writes Press, April 2016) about her journey caring for her ailing mother. Virginia has appeared on numerous television and radio programs. She holds a Fellowship in Thanatology from the Association of Death Education & Counseling (ADEC) and has been honored for her work by the cities of Indian Wells, Palm Desert, Palm Springs, and Rancho Mirage. She lives in El Dorado Hills, California with her husband Bob and her Golden Retriever Shelby.

SELECTED TITLES FROM SHE WRITES PRESS

She Writes Press is an independent publishing
company founded to serve women writers everywhere.
Visit us at www.shewritespress.com.

Don't Leave Yet: How My Mother's Alzheimer's Opened My Heart
by Constance Hanstedt. $16.95, 978-1-63152-952-8. The chronicle
of Hanstedt's journey toward independence, self-assurance, and
connectedness as she cares for her mother, who is rapidly losing her
own identity to the early stage of Alzheimer's.

Green Nails and Other Acts of Rebellion: Life After Loss by Elaine
Soloway. $16.95, 978-1-63152-919-1. An honest, often humorous
account of the joys and pains of caregiving for a loved one with a
debilitating illness.

Her Beautiful Brain: A Memoir by Ann Hedreen. $16.95, 978-1-
938314-92-6. The heartbreaking story of a daughter's experiences
as her beautiful, brainy mother begins to lose her mind to an
unforgiving disease: Alzheimer's.

***Where Have I Been All My Life? A Journey Toward Love and
Wholeness*** by Cheryl Rice. $16.95, 978-1-63152-917-7. Rice's uni-
versally relatable story of how her mother's sudden death launched
her on a journey into the deepest parts of grief—and, ultimately,
toward love and wholeness.

***Don't Call Me Mother: A Daughter's Journey from Abandonment
to Forgiveness*** by Linda Joy Myers. $16.95, 978-1-938314-02 -5. Linda
Joy Myers's story of how she transcended the prisons of her childhood
by seeking—and offering—forgiveness for her family's sins.

***Warrior Mother: A Memoir of Fierce Love, Unbearable Loss, and
Rituals that Heal*** by Sheila K. Collins, PhD. $16.95, 978-1-938314-
46-9. The story of the lengths one mother goes to when two of her
three adult children are diagnosed with potentially terminal diseases.